The Stiftung Wissenschaft und Politik (SWP) is a foundation established in 1962 for the purpose of furthering analytic research into problems of international politics and security. Publicly funded, but politically independent, the SWP today maintains the largest research institute of its kind in the Federal Republic of Germany. The SWP receives almost all of the operating funds for the institute through annual non-project appropriations from the Federal budget. These are supplemented by grants for specific projects, obtained from private foundations in the Federal Republic and abroad. The SWP's professional staff, some 45 out of a total permanent staff of 120, is drawn from a variety of disciplines and professional backgrounds.
The research activities of the SWP seek to combine the requirements of general research in international affairs with the specific needs of policymakers. To that end, the institute develops its own research agenda, giving due regard to specific questions raised by *Bundestag* members or governments departments.
Results are usually disseminated in the form of non-classified studies and position papers. Many of these are intended primarily for the attention and specific needs of policymakers. Chief recipients are the *Bundestag* and its committees, the Chancellery, and various Federal Ministries.

Aktuelle Materialien
zur Internationalen Politik

herausgegeben von der
Stiftung Wissenschaft und Politik, Ebenhausen
Redaktion: Dr. Albrecht Zunker

Band 40/4

Klaus Segbers/Stephan De Spiegeleire (Eds.)

Post-Soviet Puzzles

Mapping the Political Economy of the Former Soviet Union

Volume IV
The Emancipation of Society as a Reaction to Systemic Change: Survival, Adaptation to New Rules and Ethnopolitical Conflicts

Nomos Verlagsgesellschaft
Baden-Baden

Die Deutsche Bibliothek – CIP-Einheitsaufnahme

Post-Soviet Puzzles : Mapping the Political Economy of the Former Soviet Union / Klaus Segbers/Stephan De Spiegeleire (eds.). – Baden-Baden : Nomos Verl.-Ges.
(Aktuelle Materialien zur Internationalen Politik ; Bd. 40)
NE: Segbers, Klaus [Hrsg.]; GT
Volume 4. The Emancipation of Society as a Reaction to Systemic Change: Survival, Adaptation to New Rules and Ethnopolitical Conflicts. – 1. Aufl. – 1995
ISBN 3-7890-4045-2

1. Auflage 1995

Table of Contents

1

Ukraine's Population under Conditions of Socio-Economic Crisis: Psychological State and Factors of Survival

Evgenii Golovakha and Natal'ya Panina

In recent times the condition of Ukraine's society and state has been described by nearly all politicians, scientists and publicists as critical. As a rule, the causes and consequences of crisis are analysed in economic and political terms but the psychological factor typically remains underappreciated. The underappreciation of the role of people's psychological condition is illustrated by the fact that the psychological peculiarities of the population remain outside the scientific analysis of social processes and social forecasts.

Russia has just borne the consequences of underappreciating the role of the psychological state of the population during democratic transformations. The outcomes of election held in November 1993 shook the whole world. Democratic election led to the unexpected success of a demagogue who propagandizes fascist mottos. Most politologists found explanations for that fact, namely the impoverishment of the population and the registration of protest against the policy of economic reforms under way.

It is difficult to concur with such explanations of the outcomes of elections in Russia. If one is to adhere to the version that the fall in the people's standard of living resulting from reforms precipitated the outcomes of the latest parliamentary election, it should be admitted that it was no higher at the time of Russia's voting in favour of *Vybor Rossii*, in favour of Yeltsin or Gaidar's reforms (for example April 1993). Taking into account that the Ukrainians' standard of living is considerably lower than that of Russians, and following the hypothesis of the 'Zhirinovskii-response to impoverishment', one should have expected increased mass support of neofascist leaders. However, neither in the parliamentary nor the presidential elections in Ukraine did similar events take place.

Here, significant success was gained by the Communist Block, Socialist Block and Block of Collective Farmers' Lobby. A common feature of the situation in both

Russia and Ukraine is the political defeat of adherents of the liberal idea, most consistently defending democratic reforms. The reason for this is connected to a great extent with peculiarities of social psychology in transforming post-totalitarian society.

1 Peculiarities of the Psychological State of the Population

Empirical research conducted in the public opinion research department of the Institute of Sociology of the National Academy of Sciences of Ukraine as well as the sociological service of the 'Democratic Initiatives' centre throughout 1991-1994 on a representative nation-wide selection helps to analyse the peculiarities of the psychological state of the population in circumstances primarily characterized by a cardinal transformation of the value-and-norm system of society: declarative refusal of one system of values (socialist) which used to consolidate the social system and refusal to set up a new one. Our results, despite their empirical reference to Ukraine, can characterize common processes inherent in sharp transformation of social systems in general.

1.1 Anomie: Mass Demoralization and Social Superfluity

When Ukraine declared its independence in 1991, on the basis of which the construction of a new state and new society was started, the creation of democratic principles in politics and economics was proclaimed as a basic aim. The outcomes of sociological studies showed the majority of people supporting the goal[1].

Thus, at the first stage of building democratic society, the political leadership declared and the majority of the population supported the rejection of totalitarian principles of state building and acceptance of new democratic ones. However, the value-goals declared never became real regulators of social life because they were not fortified by appropriate institutionalized norms. Consequently, the condition of *anomie* set in (i.e., one value-and-norm system collapsed, and was not replaced by another), resulting in mass spread of anomic demoralization.

---

1 Golovakha, E. „Political consciousness, legitimacy and personality: transition from totalitarism to democracy in Ukraine." In *Integrating political science, socialisation and education: international perspectives for the next century.* R. Farnen (ed.). Oldenburg: University, 1993: 139-152.

The data of a representative survey of Ukraine's population we received in April 1992[2] revealed that anomie caused a high rate of demoralization in practically all strata of Ukraine's population. The research employed a special method for measuring the level of demoralization caused by the overall response to anomie.

The scale of anomic demoralization was devised on the basis of McClousky-Srole's method, adapted by N. Popov and tested by the authors in July 1991 on a representative selection of Kiev's population. The scale includes 9 reasoning points concerning assessments of stability of common social norms as well as personal condition with dichotomic scale of answers. The 'agree' answer equalled 2 points, 'disagree' – 0 points, 'hard to say' – 1 point. The overall index ranged from 0 to 18 points, where 0 stands for entire negation of anomie's demoralizing influence, 9 points represent the zero mark on the scale, and figures above indicate the degree of anomic demoralization, and 18 points show the ultimate rate of demoralization of society.

The data obtained enabled us to draw the conclusion that in April 1992 anomie had caused a high rate of demoralization in practically all strata of Ukraine's population. The average demoralization index equalled 13.5 points; some demoralization was observed in 85% of the population. A comparative study of different categories of the population showed that despite certain differences (e.g. the lower the age and the higher the educational level, the lower the demoralization rate), no socio-demographic group of the population had an index figure of less than 12 points (index of anomic demoralization of students).

Examination of the relationship between people's demoralization and their socio-political orientations (as prerequisites for the formation of a value-and-norm system) showed that individuals oriented towards a capitalist course of development and the introduction of market principles of economy are demoralized to a lesser extent than those oriented towards the old ideological system (socialist principles of state formation) or those unable to define their own socio-political position. Thus, orientations towards new value-goals help to some extent to overcome demoralization which is brought about by the destruction of the former foundations of value-and-norm regulation. However, the study of orientations towards various means of setting up and promoting new values revealed that people who are not afflicted by anomic demoralization are more likely to resort to illegitimate means of

---

2 Held by the public opinion research department of the Institute of Sociology of the National Academy of Sciences of Ukraine using a programme elaborated by the authors of the report, in which 1752 individuals in all regions of the country were polled.

struggle for their interests (unauthorized strikes, occupation of buildings, creation of illegal armed formations, etc.).

Hence, the absence of demoralization itself is not indicative of an absence of the destructive influence of anomie. A situation characterized by the acceptance of a value-goal but not of institutionalized values of how to achieve that goal regarded by R. Merton as anomie itself following the example of American society in the 1920-30s. We consider this to be one of the possible types of response to anomie, an non-normative response to anomie, so to say, i.e., indifference to the means of reaching an objective.

Internalized lack of prejudice towards the means of reaching an objective (or more exactly, towards norms) leads to the formation of cynicism, which is one of the forms of response to anomie and the state of demoralization induced by anomie. Demoralization is closely connected with the feeling of *social superfluity* by which we mean the degree of an individual's satisfaction with his/her walk of life, as well as satisfaction with that which he/she receives from society and what he/she is able to contribute to society under specific conditions of social activity. In this respect Table 1 provides data on the elements of people's contentment with their interrelations with society (Table 1).

Table 1 *Satisfaction of Ukrainian citizens with their walk of life (according to survey data, May-June 1994. N=1807), %*

Questions about satisfaction	Level of satisfaction		
	Generally satisfied	Hard to say	Generally unsatisfied
Are you currently satisfied with your walk of life?	12.6	24.9	62.5
To what extent are you satisfied with what you receive from society?	6.1	28.5	65.4
To what extent are you satisfied with what you contribute society?	16.0	27.2	56.8

It is evident that the majority of Ukraine's population experience a feeling of dissatisfaction with their position within the transforming society. This feeling appeared, however, in the first year of Ukraine's independence and has not changed dramatically since then. Thus, according to the poll in April 1992, only 16% were satisfied with their position in society overall, 25% were satisfied with what they contribute to society and 9% with what they receive from it.

At the same time, the majority see themselves as being quite low down on the social ladder. When asked to place themselves within a hypothetical hierarchy consisting of seven 'rungs', Ukrainian residents from various walks of life tended to place themselves on the lowest social rungs. The first rung (the lowest) was chosen by 19.7%, the second one – 25.6%, the third one – 32.8%, the fourth one – 18.9%, the fifth one – 2.2%. the sixth – 0.4%, the seventh one (the highest) – 0.4%. Overall, over three-quarters of the Ukrainian population see themselves as occupying the lower rungs of the social ladder, while only 3% move on to those rungs lying above the 'golden mean'.

The question arises: perhaps most people are satisfied with the situation? On the lower rungs social responsibility is less. Perhaps people do not want to move upwards from the place they see themselves as currently occupying? However, the data on overall dissatisfaction of most people with their social position refute such an assumption.

It was originally supposed that social superfluity would be higher among senior generations than among young and middle-aged people, and higher among unemployed individuals than among employed ones (as is usually the case in stable societies). However, the data obtained refute these hypotheses: social superfluity prevails in nearly all population groups in Ukraine. Thus, in a society that declared the building of democracy there are practically no significantly large social groups within the overall structure of the population which could identify themselves with society and feel needed and useful in its transformation.

However, even without conducting special studies on the dimensions of the demoralization rate and the social usefulness of population, the high rate of this state may be inferred from certain manifestations of mass consciousness. One of the indicators is the growth of apocalyptic moods and utterances. Widespread feelings of 'disaster' and 'calamity' as apparent or even as already having happened can be regarded as indicative of demoralization, causing the need for a normative response to the anomie.

1.2 Responses to Anomie: Threat of Return to Paternalism

Anomie cannot continue unabated within society because under such conditions the underlying mechanisms of social consolidation are demolished. Two responses to anomie arise within the mass consciousness – *a normative* and *a non-normative one*. The non-normative response to anomie is the formation of a dismissive attitude towards norms as means of achieving goals. Normlessness in this instance is itself accepted as a norm of behaviour. The second response to anomie is a normative reaction, characterized by a desperate need of the establishment of some manner of norms.

The non-normative response is sub-divided into two basic types:

- *Cynicism* – the tendency to regard *any* means of achieving a goal as acceptable.
- *Agressive and extremist tendencies* – regarding violent means as especially good since they allow one to achieve a goal in the quickest possible way.

The normative response also has two basic versions:

- Formation of orientations towards '*a return to the past*'
- Formation of the '*need to bring a strong personality to power*', who will be able to establish a 'new stringent order'.

What types of tendencies are forming among the Ukrainian population under conditions of prolonged anomie? As far as the spread of extremism is concerned, nowadays most people stand for non-violent, legitimate forms of protest: the more violent an action looks, the fewer people take to it[3]. However, a close connection has been discovered between the rate of anomic demoralization and aggressive moods or orientation towards extremist measures. There are not very many people in Ukraine who are personally prepared to take violent actions, but the number of those supporting such measures is increasing. For instance, people suffering from an extremely high level of demoralization consider involvement of the Army, Afghanistan veterans and the use of force and weapons to be the best measures in order to crack down on violent crime[4]. The number of people who regard armed skirmishes in Ukraine as being possible is rising dramatically, from 4% in 1990 up to 54% in 1993.

As far as cynicism is concerned, our data show that it is becoming fairly spread on the grounds of anomic demoralization, and is used as a psychological defence *against* anomie demoralization, yet it is characterized as being not very pronounced: 51% are subject to a low degree of cynicism, 31% – a medium degree, and 18% – a high degree.

An increase in the degree of cynicism can, unfortunately, be observed in people oriented towards building up a democratic state (according to the Western model). We believe this can be explained by the fact that the idea of institutionalized democratic norms as a means of achieving an appropriate goal has not formed among these people.

---

3 Golovakha, E. and N. Panina N. „The Development of a Democratic Political Identity in Contemporary Ukrainian Political Culture." In *Nationalism, Ethnicity and Identity. Cross-National and Comparative Perspectives*. Farnen, Russell F. (ed.). New Brunswick, N.J.: Transaction Publishers, 1994.

4 Golovakha, E., and N. Panina. „Democratization and Culture of Law of a Personality," *Philosophic and Sociological Thought* 1992, no. 8: 3-11.

Today, however, the Ukrainian population mostly tends to display the normative response to anomie, which is expressed through anomic nostalgia for 'the past'. Nostalgia for the abstract past 'when society had a definite order', represents quite a serious emotional basis for supporting specific political programmes aimed at returning to practically any of the previous political systems, if political forces of significant authority advocate them.

In this case there is a possible return to either an archaic and traditional society or a socialist one. Prerequisites for a return to an archaic and traditional society can actually be traced in those data revealing a psychological insulation from other peoples – a peculiar form of egocentrism. According to the Bogardus scale of social distance, Ukraine's population rejects practically all nationalities except for the traditional residents of Ukrainian territory: Ukrainians, Russians, Belorussians and Jews[5].

However, a return to the values of socialist society is more likely. The socialist and communist systems are rejected by the population as terms, but paternalistic tendencies and convictions – the value basis of the socialist system – are widespread among the population.

Currently most people adhere to the opinion that it is the state's obligation to provide them with the necessary material wealth, and do not see any great prospects in the idea of solving material problems by means of individual economic and political initiative. Thus, according to the results of the poll held in May-June 1994, only 12% believe they can undertake some form of action if local authorities make a decision that is counter to the people's interests; even fewer (6%) consider that they be able to do anything if a clamp-down decision is enacted by Ukraine's government (in the poll in 1991 the proportions were 13% and 9% respectively).

Paternalism, which was fostered by the communist system of socialization, is a serious value basis for a return to communist principles for the organization of society. Nowadays, communist values as the goal of social development have been declaratively rejected by most people; however a considerable upsurge in the number of people ready to accept the communist-socialist platform as a basic objective for the formation of society has been observed. As early as 1992-1993, communist and socialist trends in the political arena were backed by 2-4% of the Ukrainian population, but judging by the results of a study conducted in May-June 1994, these trends are supported by 10% and 11% respectively. These tendencies are

5 Golovakha, E., and N. Panina. *Social insanity. History, Theory and Contemporary Practice*. Kiev: Abris, 1994: 168.

particularly strong in Eastern Ukraine, where a strengthening of similar political orientations has already led to the communists prevailing in the elections to Ukraine's Supreme Council (Table 2).

Table 2 *Regional features of the political orientations of the Ukrainian population (according to survey data from May-June 1994, N=1807)*

	Kiev	West	Centre	East	South	Crimea	Ukraine
Communist	5.6	3.8	10.3	15.5	7.5	7.9	10.5
Socialist	7.8	2.8	8.7	15.5	12.6	14.6	10.8
Social-Democratic	6.7	2.8	4.9	5.0	3.1	16.9	5.1
Nationalist	5.6	5.9	1.3	0.8	0.6	0.0	2.0
National-Democratic	10.0	16.9	4.7	3.2	4.4	3.4	6.5
Liberal	6.7	0.6	0.7	2.1	4.4	1.1	1.9
Anarchic, Anarcho-syndicalist	2.2	0.6	0.2	0.8	0.0	1.1	0.6
Religious (fundamentalist)	1.1	3.8	0.9	0.6	3.1	0.0	1.5
Christian-Democratic	3.3	5.6	2.5	2.4	5.0	4.5	3.4
Others	3.3	0.6	1.3	0.8	0.0	0.0	0.9
None of them	18.9	15.0	13.6	10.2	12.6	6.7	12.4
Still have not decided	18.9	16.2	19.0	18.2	19.5	14.6	18.0
I am not familiar with these	12.2	25.6	32.4	26.9	28.3	32.6	27.7
TOTAL	100	100	100	100	100	100	100

N.B. The survey was conducted in those regions of Ukraine defined according to geopolitical peculiarities in the mass consciousness of the population. As a result of grouping the *oblast*'s according to these features, six regions were defined, among which Ukraine's capital was presented separately. In every region the number of people polled reflects the proportion of their regional population within the population of the whole of Ukraine. Additionally, the study observed the quota principle of sampling according to sex, age and education in conformity with regional peculiarities of these socio-demographic features. Regions: 1.Kiev; 2.Western (Volyn, Roven, Ivano-Frankovsk, Lvov, Ternopol, Transcarpathians, Chernovtsy); 3.Central (Zhytomir, Chernigov, Kiev region – without Kiev, Vinnitsa, Kirovograd, Poltava, Cherkassy, Khmelnitsky); 4.Eastern (Sumy, Kharkov, Donetsk, Lugansk, Dnepropetrovsk, Zaporozhie); 5.Southern (Nikolaev, Odessa, Kherson); 6.The Crimea

Summing up the outcomes of the study of the psychological state of the population under conditions of anomie and value formation under these conditions, it should be noted that in the case of the Ukrainian population, the normative response to anomie is absolutely prevalent, which inevitably leads to the formation of totalitarian orientations: traditional archaic, socialist or authoritarian fascist.

Taking into account widely spread orientations towards paternalistic values/means, at the end of 1992 one could already forecast rivalry between orientations towards a right-wing authoritarian society (with a powerful authoritarian leader) and a left-wing authoritarian society (communist and socialist). If in 1993 in Ukraine a political figure conforming to the mass idea of a powerful leader had appeared, a serious authoritarian fascist threat could have emerged in Ukraine as was the case in Russia at the time.

However, Ukrainian citizens have not yet found such a leader (less than one-fifth of Ukraine's population believe that today there are political leaders able to run the country effectively). Under conditions of anomie, while searching for some value-and-norm basis (essential for proper social interaction), the population's mass consciousness starts increasingly coming out in favour of political forces that declare socialism as an underlying value-goal of further social development.

2 Factors of Survival of the Population under Anomie

Ukraine turned out to be one of the few FSU republics that managed to avoid irreconcilable confrontation between miscellaneous political forces and bloody conflicts. This quite paradoxical (under conditions of the deepest economic slump) political phenomenon deserves special attention.

2.1 What is the Value of the First Years of 'Survival' ?

In principle, it cannot be ruled out that Ukraine has been accumulating experience in moving peacefully from communist dictatorship and planned economy to open democratic society. This would be a unique experience of great current and historic value that is worth reproducing in other countries denying their communist past. Perhaps the price for 'conflictlessness' at the first stage of independent existence – economic collapse and mass demoralization – is not so high that one must reject the chosen strategy of development that ensures a 'lean peace', which is known to be better than a 'good war'.

The Soviet Union, however, also used to preserve peace and tranquility within its frontiers during the years of 'stagnation', which nevertheless did not prevent either the loss of its superpower aureole or the emergence of numerous regional conflicts resulting from gradual socio-economic degradation. Nor did this internal peace and tranquility avert the Soviet Union's overall departure from the geopolitical arena as a state, becoming an object of historic analysis under the currently accepted title 'the former Soviet Union'.

This reason alone should give cause to a sceptical assessment of the two to three years' relative peace in Ukraine following the declaration of its independence. One should not forget that during the domination of a totalitarian system, the Soviet Union was in possession of certain means of preventing open social conflicts which are not available to Ukraine's governing elite. It is one thing to deal with malcontents and rebels under conditions of overall fear of political persecution by the authorities and quite another to attempt to prevent a social outbreak in society where open manifestation of dissatisfaction, rejection of power and outright xenophobia are becoming quite a 'natural' and considerably widespread manifestation of social activity, rather than a bold, isolated challenge to the system.

Under these conditions it would be natural to expect open vertical (power and people) and horizontal (interelitarian and egalitarian) conflicts in Ukraine as can be observed in a number of other post-communist states which rejected the old social system and found themselves in a deep socio-economic crisis. In Ukraine, however, there are prerequisites for preventing wide-scale destructive conflicts which are linked with the factors of survival and the reorganization of society; factors resisting the destabilizing impact of socio-economic crisis and anomie.

Of these factors one should immediately single out the intrapolitical course of the authorities, who managed to utilize the totalitarian experience of ruling society in the new conditions by setting up a particular *'Ukrainian model'* of post-totalitarian social development and by capitalizing on Ukraine's non-acceptance of violence as a way of solving political and economic contradictions, even if they substantially deteriorate conditions of daily life.

The second factor is stipulated by the paradoxical phenomenon of '*social security against the state*' which, unlike traditional legal security, develops through the complete incapability of the state to demand from its citizens the fulfilment of ineffective, contradictory or under-institutionalized legislation.

The third factor is connected to the so-called '*people's economy*' which appeared as a counterweight to the dilapidated state-and-collective-farm economy, and provided a subsistence wage for the majority of the population under conditions when public salaries, pensions and grants do not suffice even for basic physical survival.

2.2 The 'Ukrainian Model' of Post-Totalitarian Survival

The essence of the 'Ukrainian model' of post-totalitarian development is determined by the authorities' aspiration to maintain the social balance by means of minimizing social upheavals and preserving old structures and mechanisms of social control, thus preventing the mass social superfluity which is an inevitable consequence of a structural social change. The outcome of the realization of this model is on the one hand the absence of wide-scale violent conflicts and on the other, complete recession in the economy and in socio-political activity. To gain mass support for such a strategy, a total fear of any conflict is cultivated in society, which inevitably also covers the conflict that is necessary for democratic development – the conflict between the dying totalitarian structures of control and civil society. As a result, people's fear of constructive social conflicts becomes itself a mechanism hampering any constructive steps towards overcoming the socio-economic crisis.

Being fairly intimidated by the idea of probable social chaos arising through radicalization of social changes, most people adhere to the same 'political line' that the power structures adhere to: decoratively coming out in favour of ideas of social democratization, market reform and building up of a state founded on law, they undertake nothing to actually achieve these political goals, neither trusting politicians nor insisting on a fully active implementation of their efforts to create a democratic state with an efficient market economy. This fear, being common to both the old governing elite which is afraid of losing its customary levers of control as well as to the 'silent majority', which clings to this elite and sees in its customary administrative and regulatory appearance a guarantor of the 'lean peace', is a main source of economic degradation and of discrediting the idea of state independence.

Being afraid of civil war and violence, the residents of all Ukrainian regions prefer to patiently endure the hardships caused by mismanagement of the economy, if this is the price they believe they have to pay in order to preserve peace in the country. This is the conclusion produced by the data set out in the table 3.

Table 3 *Distribution of answers among the population of different Ukrainian regions to the question „What do you think is better – to endure any material hardships for the sake of order, peace and calm in the country or in the event of a significant deterioration of living conditions to take to the street in a protest ?" (according to survey data May-June 1994, N=1807)*

	Kiev	West	Centre	East	South	Crimea	Ukraine
One should preserve order, peace and consent at any cost	34.4	54.2	48.6	37.4	49.4	50.6	44.9
Hard to say	37.8	22.7	32.5	36.6	31.0	19.1	31.7
One should actively protest against constant deterioration of living conditions	27.8	23.1	18.9	26.0	19.6	30.3	23.4
TOTAL	100	100	100	100	100	100	100

A similar model of post-totalitarian survival was accepted in a number of other countries that appeared after the USSR's collapse, primarily Belarus and Kazakhstan, their political and economic stance having many common features. The difference consists in their greater aspirations towards integration with Russia, as well as in the stronger influence of the old *nomenclatura* and paternalistic orientations in Ukraine. Therefore it can be surmised that reforms in these states will be dependent to a greater extent on the situation in Russia. If antidemocratic forces prevail or isolationist tendencies strengthen in Russia, economic reforms in Belarus and Kazakhstan will practically come to a halt. Ukraine, however, on the strength of a more evolved political pluralism is in a position to carry out economical reforms independently. The success of a determined turn to reforms as proclaimed by Ukraine's president L.Kuchma will depend on whether existing factors of survival suffice to offset the denial of state paternalism and the 'conflictless strategy'.

2.3 The phenomenon of 'security by means of lawlessness'

In recent years, the social security of the population has been a leitmotiv of political discussions in post-communist countries. Liberals who are in favour of a market economy are primarily being accused of demolishing by their reforms the system of social protection of the population which allegedly existed in the socialist state. Avoiding a discussion about the natural or perverted essence of the totalitarian system of social protection of the population, it has to be emphasized that post-totalitarian society set up a no less refined system of social protection which is given an undeservedly low level of coverage in the discussion of social security issues. As a counterweight to the common public defencelessness inherent in a bankrupt state, a substitute mechanism of citizens' self-defence against an incompetent state system has emerged. The essence of this mechanism consists in the substitution of the basic organizational principle of a democratic society – 'everybody is equal before the law' – with the principle that 'everybody is equal before the lawlessness'. Building on this principle, the population considers the country to be ruled chiefly by mafia and regards it as their 'civil duty' to confront 'that mafia' by means of tax evasion, smuggling goods banned by customs regulations out of Ukraine, etc.

Moreover, the residents of all regions of Ukraine attribute a leading position to the mafia in building up the state (table 4).

Table 4 *Distribution of answers among the population of different Ukrainian regions to the question „What social groups do you think play a considerable role in state building in Ukraine?" (according to survey data May-June 1994, N=1807),%*

	Kiev	West	Centre	East	South	Crimea	Ukraine
Workers	12.2	25.2	25.4	27.4	17.6	5.6	23.7
Peasants	12.2	25.5	23.6	22.2	15.1	5.6	21.2
Intellectuals	10.0	21.7	13.1	17.7	16.4	11.1	16.4
Businessmen, entrepreneurs	24.4	29.5	21.8	24.1	21.4	27.8	24.5
Enterprise managers	16.9	15.5	16.0	16.5	16.4	13.3	16.0
Civil servants	25.6	26.1	30.3	29.2	33.3	28.9	29.1
Pensioners	0.0	1.6	1.6	2.7	1.9	1.1	1.9
Directors of collective and state farms	2.2	12.7	12.9	10.3	10.1	6.7	10.8
Politicians-democrats	15.6	20.2	7.8	7.7	10.1	2.2	10.3
Politicians-communists	10.0	18.3	8.5	11.8	13.3	1.1	11.7
Politicians-nationalists	13.3	14.9	5.3	7.6	10.7	35.6	10.3
Military people	1.1	8.1	6.2	6.8	9.4	3.3	6.7
Police and security officials	5.6	8.4	4.9	10.3	8.8	4.4	7.9
Mafia, underworld	36.7	30.1	29.4	35.9	38.4	44.4	33.9
Others	2.2	0.0	0.4	1.0	0.6	0.0	0.7
Nobody	5.6	5.3	4.7	3.4	4.4	2.2	4.2
Hard to say	17.8	17.7	19.8	15.9	13.8	23.3	17.5
TOTAL	100	100	100	100	100	100	100

Even in Western Ukraine, where the idea of priority of national statehood building has the deepest roots, disappointment with the current course of development of statehood in Ukraine is displayed to exactly the same extent as in 'Russified' Eastern Ukraine. Futhermore, the more people link the public and political process with the interests of mafia circles, the more they take a completely individualistic stand on the possibility of personal survival under common degradation. One of the manifestations of such reorientation in the economy is the phenomenon of increasing development of the 'people's economy' against a background of the collapse of the macroeconomic system.

2.4 The Factor of the 'People's Economy'

Among the factors ensuring physical survival and moderating the manifestation of mass discontent and protest, one should first of all single out the phenomenon of self-arrangement of the economic life of the population under conditions of the collapse of the 'big economy'. Here, the natural economy, which partially provides three quarters of Ukrainian residents with foodstuff, and small trade resulting from trips by one quarter of the population out of the country (survey data, May 1994) enable the majority not to sink to the poverty line, below which civil disobedience, spontaneus aggression and readiness to support extremism set in.

The overwhelming majority of Ukrainian citizens are of the opinion that there are currently two sections of the population that live better now than in the past. This is revealed by the data of one all-Ukrainian poll held in June, 1993. Table 5 shows the distribution of answers to the question „How do you think the position of the following strata has changed since Ukraine gained independence ?"

Table 5 *Assessment by the Ukrainian population of the change in the position of social strata after the declaration of independence (according to survey data, June 1993, N=1797),%*

Social strata	Position			
	improved	*remained unchanged*	*deteriorated*	*hard to say*
Pensioners	91.7	4.3	1.9	2.1
Workers	84.8	8.7	2.6	1.9
Peasants	77.3	10.9	5.0	7.8
Intellectuals	63.1	14.2	7.0	15.7
Entrepreneurs	6.1	9.1	73.7	11.1
High officials	2.4	13.7	74.5	9.4

As one can see, the population shows no particular difference of opinion on the question „Who lives well in Ukraine ?" Every-one was deemed to be worse off, except for highly-placed officials for whom it would have been a sin to deteriorate their own position, and also entrepreneurs, who somehow unexpectedly broke through the permanent restrictions on so badly needed economic freedoms imposed for the last two years. Under the economic policy of recent years, a particular stratum of entrepreneurs is soon likely to emerge in Ukraine who will finally realize that they should lead an inconspicuous way of life so as not to let the population distinguish them from the poor social strata, and who will purposefully start going bankrupt together with the state economy (which is good at this). Even so, a different outcome seems more likely, one which is more appropriate to the logic of the world historic development of entrepreneurship: domestic businessmen will wish to live better than they did up to now and will try to steer the political situation and public opinion towards the idea that is simple yet hard for mass consciousness to accept, that any country will live more affluently, the more entrepreneurs and their businesses prosper in it.

It is not the extent to which the masses take to this idea, or the preference shown to entrepreneurship by the present authorities that will primarily determine the future of private entreprise in Ukraine but rather the future political and economic outlook of the country and its prospects of finding a way out of the current socio-economic impasse.

It is safe to say that the probability of a social outbreak in the nearest future will increase, the more state barriers are put in the way of the development of the 'people's economy' and above all the more hindrances are placed on the small enterprise now in spontaneous formation. Generally it is hard to imagine by what means, besides outright totalitarian terror, the drive to individual economic initiative can be hindered now it has emerged in society.

This very factor, relative freedom of small enterprising, chiefly defines the ability of a considerable part of the population to survive under macroeconomic collapse. At the same time, economic activity of this kind also contributes to the prevention of tumultuous forms of destructive social protest, diverting the most active and mobile part of population from violent forms of protest and making it possible to avoid deficits and 'hunger lines' which are potential sources of concentration and boisterous manifestation of mass discontent. Young people prevail in small business and the majority of them, unlike senior generations, approve the idea of final denial of socialist paternalism and stand for a transition to an economy that builds on private property. This circumstance determines our optimistic assessment of the outlook for the phasing in of a market economy in Ukraine which could serve as a basis for strengthening the currently nascent political democracy.

3 Conclusions

In conclusion we would like to emphasise that optimistic forecasts of Ukraine's development and substitutions of the above-mentioned survival factors for normal, civilized socio-economic mechanisms are presented as a relatively long-term perspective of social development. As far as the nearest future is concerned, optimism can be at best moderate taking into account actual threats to democratic refinements caused by the prevailing psychological background of anomic demoralization and totalitarian-nostalgic responses to it. In this connection, the question of social mechanisms for preventing further spread of demoralization in society and disappointment with democratic norms and values requires particular consideration.

It is easy to notice that all survival factors we have considered are connected more with 'defensive regression' of people (including people in power) than with rational attempts to significantly improve the socio-political situation. That is the source of the limited prospects for containing catastrophic tendencies. Another couple of years of such 'self-defence' and the situation in Ukraine will be not far from apocalyptic. For this reason, economic reforms in Ukraine should be carried out according to the same stringent guidelines that Poland and, to an extent, Russia once decided to follow.

The orientation towards drastic reforms declared by the current president is perhaps the last chance for reformers to win some support of the population in this century. Failure in this attempt at economic reform may hinder the democratic development of Ukraine for a decade. In this connection, assistance from the West at this stage of Ukraine's development becomes of paramount importance, not only for further maintenance of the standard of living which is indispensable to the elementary survival of the poor, but also in order to eliminate the situation where the majority of the population are impoverished because of the incompetence of the authorities and residual paternalistic stereotypes of mass consciousness.

2

Poverty in Modern Russia: Strategies of Survival and Strategies of Research

Viktor Voronkov

In September 1994, in compliance with the order of the President of Russia the country's first ever 'anti-poverty programme' was to have been completed. This programme is an official acknowledgement of the fact that poverty today is one of Russia's most crucial social problems. Along with other things, the programme should give a precise definition of poverty in Russia and help to assess its real scale.

A number of interviews with and addresses by officials and designers of the programme give us sufficient grounds to assert that as its basis the programme will have an administrative concept of poverty. This means that separate social groups will be identified such as elderly people as well as incapacitated persons and the jobless, also unmarried mothers, persons with low income and families with many children, and social aid will be given to those categories which will thus become the programme's main object.

The administrative concept of poverty means that the State itself determines the categories of the needy, instead of addressing the plight of the poor regardless of the social group they belong to. Nevertheless, the basic idea of the programme is well-grounded. Indeed, the percentage of the poor in those groups is higher than in any other comparable groups, because the former are much more vulnerable to the risks connected with the emerging market's competitive environment.[1]

Under the present conditions, any other approach to the problem of poverty is unlikely because this problem has never undergone any statistical analysis. The very existence of poverty was until quite recently denied for ideological reasons.[2] Therefore there are no objective data upon which the programme could be based.

---

1 Oyen, Else. "Some Basic Issues in the Comparative Poverty Research." *International Social Science Journal* 44, no. 4 (November 1992): 615-626.

2 "In the early 1930s it was declared that the foundation of socialism had been laid and, accordingly, causes of poverty had been eradicated... calculations were cancelled and restored

Unfortunately, even now there are no thorough studies of poverty and of its causes and scale in Russia. Subjective approaches based on feelings rather than on scientific research are predominant today. Experts of different 'party' orientations very rarely show their concern for a true representation of reality. The most typical form of scientific craftiness is the exaggeration of one symptom and the underestimation of the other.

This is most vividly demonstrated by the estimates of poverty given by different specialists when they try to identify the proportion of those with the minimal income per capita. Their estimates vary from 8% to 80% for the whole population![3] Some experts maintain that real money income has dropped by one third this year,[4] others cite quite different data that prove to the contrary that real income has grown considerably (by 10%) and that many other indicators of the living standards of the whole population also show an improvement.[5]

Such discrepancies in the estimates of the present situation result not only from the different methods of research, but also from the vacuum in which the researchers studying public welfare work. Theoretical models and concepts like 'work in the public (state) economy is the only source of well-being', that have been in wide use until quite recently, are all gone now. The concept of the constant growth of the proportion of the goods provided to an individual by so-called public consumption funds (free medical assistance, free education and kindergartens, and free housing) has also lost all its meaning.

There is an assumption that along with the common external features of poverty such as low income as well as the absence of savings, and prevailing expenditures on food rather than on other goods, poverty in Russia has many essentially different social features than poverty in the countries with a developed market economy.

D. Berto has made a very shrewd observation in this connection, which should serve as a warning to those researchers and politicians who consider different

---

only in the 1960s... And the results of research in this field were classified." Yarygina T. "Poverty in Rich Russia." *Social Sciences and Modern Times* 1994, no. 2: 28.

3 Some important illustrations: in a semester report by the *Institute of Social and Political Studies* it is stated than the poor in Russia are no less than 80% of the whole population. (Arifgianov, R. "A Well-to-Do Person Turns into a Poor One as Number of Mercedes and Beggars Grows." *Izvestia* 15 September 1994). According to the estimates by the *Centre of Economic Conjuncture* in 1993 36-38% lived below the poverty line (*Nezavisimaya Gazeta* 3 February 1994). Another expert gives 9.4% (Gelbras, V. "The Four Myths about the Situation of Workers in Russia." *Obschaya Gazeta* 24 June 1994).

4 Arifgianov, "A Well-to-Do Turns Poor."

5 Illarionov, A. "Drop in Living Standards: Myth or Reality?" *Izvestia* 17 February 1994.

phenomena to be the same judging by their apparent external resemblance. Analysing the biography of a worker's family, D. Berto arrives at the conclusion that "although Russian cities resemble clusters of multi-storeyed boxes so well-known by the people of Western Europe, they are essentially different from European cities from the point of view of the system of social relations concealed in them".[6]

It is impossible to form an adequate understanding of poverty in Russia as a social phenomenon (which is something more than its external manifestation) without revealing the essence of those social relations. In this respect, it is very important to ascertain the role of major social institutions and norms that stipulated in the past permissible modes of securing certain living standards for every person in the former Soviet Union. In other words, we must determine which of the old mechanisms continue to indirectly affect Russian society through the socialisation of several generations of Soviet people.

Under the former social system, the majority of the population preferred to stick to one universal pattern of behaviour. Under that system, the living standard of a person did not depend on his or her efforts, but were determined by special measures taken by the State in order to improve those standards. Wages did not depend on the value of produced goods nor on economic profitability of production. Wage rates and salaries of certain categories of workers and in certain branches of economy were periodically reconsidered and changed by government decisions. The salary received by different categories of workers was decided by the authorities regardless of the value of the goods they produced, which naturally, varied between industries.

People could obtain goods and certain privileges only in the form of grants from the State, through which the State rewarded compliance with a system of formal rules (such as a long-term residence in one place and a long-term service at one place of employment and so forth). Generosity of those grants depended on the means of the State or of the enterprise at which a person worked. Personal efforts and aspirations did not practically affect an individual's level of material well-being.

In general, personal well-being that was above the average level was viewed with suspicion by society in general, as something almost indecent. Thus, for example, for the *nomenklatura* (officials of all levels in the former USSR) there was a system of sanctions punishing actions that qualified as 'indecent behaviour'. Any kind of well-being exceeding standards approved by society in general and often formally

6 Berto D. and M. Malisheva. *Cultural Model of Russian Population and a Forced Transition to the Market. Biographical Methodology – History, Methodology, Practice.* Moscow: Institute of Sociology RAN, 1994: 101.

and juridically fixed standards (top salary limits, living space limits, restrictions on the norms of possession of land, norms regulating possession of a private car and immovables, a ban on private ownership means of production) aroused suspicions of so-called 'unearned income'. The mere fact of possessing property exceeding publicly accepted limits provided sufficient grounds for taking up criminal proceedings against the owner. State policy in the sphere of regulation of the well-being of the population was characterised by frequent campaigns against 'unearned incomes'.

As a result of such policy, households officially regarded as poor and those relatively well-to-do did not practically differ from each other according to a number of indicators of prosperity, as is shown in a survey conducted in 1991. The following indicators of living standards such as living space and possession of durable goods (refrigerators, washing machines, TV sets, vacuum cleaners and even cars) were practically equal in both categories of households.[7] The same survey places the majority of the working population in the low income groups – a fact that is very characteristic of our conditions.

Naturally, a specific mode (strategy) of economic as well as socio-political and everyday behaviour emerged which became the most characteristic feature of the so-called '*homo sovieticus*'. This strategy as an optimal mode of behaviour under the given conditions, consists in *minimising* efforts made in order to obtain a predetermined amount and type of reward (generally speaking, totally unrelated to those efforts) for one's participation in the activities of different public institutions.

The whole cluster of conditions stipulating rigid limits to the possible level of well-being, as well as the minimising of permissible means of achieving it, has created a specific 'socialist way of life' as an ideological standard. Modest income and personal poverty had been cultivated as a publicly approved moral merit. Transition from that general condition of society to other social and cultural patterns, which is now taking place under the pressure of the current social and economic reforms, gives us a unique opportunity for scientific research.

Today, we do not yet have all the necessary theoretical tools and methods to conduct this research. As is shown in some recent studies, traditional methods of studying poverty "are undergoing a crisis both with respect to theoretical tools and

7 Yarygina, T. "Poverty in Rich Russia.": 30.

with respect to tools of a 'general welfare state'".[8] A widely-known Norwegian researcher on poverty, Else Oyen, asserts that "there is not a single universal or at least a predominant theory of poverty today, and it is unlikely that such a theory will ever be created".[9]

The theoretical model that is most adequate and applicable to the phenomenon of poverty in Russia is, in our opinion, a synthesis of approaches being developed in the classical theories of disorganisation[10] as well as in the theory of anomie[11] and in that of the 'culture of poverty'[12] and in socio-economics.[13]

Thus, the theory of disorganisation describes precisely that condition of society that we can observe now in Russia, i.e., vagueness of norms regulating behaviour of the majority of the Russian population. In particular, disorganisation entails the loss of the usual and traditional patterns of behaviour. On the other hand, the present condition of anomie embracing Russian society reflects a discrepancy well-elaborated in the theory of anomie between the goals pursued by society and the means of achieving them. At the same time, poverty as such is not the central subject of research in those theories, so they should be complemented with specific concepts of a different level.

With regard to the subject of our research, the most adequate theory for describing and revealing the specific character of Russian poverty and the reasons for its preservation is that of the 'culture of poverty'.[14] However, in our opinion, this theory has one essential defect that narrows its application to Russia, namely its static character. Within the framework of this theory, poverty is regarded as a product of culture, as a certain subculture within the broader context of the predominant cultural dimension. That subculture represents a specific way of life

---

8 Guidicini P. and Pieretti G. *Le radici dell'impoverimento: Tessute sociale, famiglia e poverta a Bologna negli anni 90.* Milano: France Angeli, 1992 (quoted by: "Social Sciences Abroad." *Sociology* 1993, no. 2: 71).

9 Oyen E. "Some Basic Issues.": 215.

10 Cooley, C. *Human nature and the social order.* New York: C. Scribner's sons, 1902; Thomas, William Isaac and Florian Znaniecki. *The Polish peasant in Europe and America.* New York: Knopf, 1927; Cohen, Morris Raphael. *Reason and nature; an essay on the meaning of scientific method.* Glencoe, Ill.: Free Press, 1959; and others.

11 Durkheim, Emile. *Le suicide; étude de sociologie.* Paris: F. Alcan, 1897; Merton, Robert King. *Social theory and social structure.* Glencoe, Ill.: Free Press, 1957; and others.

12 Lewis, Oscar. *Five families: Mexican case studies in the culture of poverty.* New York: Basic Books, 1975 and others.

13 Etzioni, Amitai. "How Is Russia Bearing up?" *Challenge* 35, no. 3 (May-June 1992): 40-43.

14 Yaroshenko, S. "Poverty Syndrome." *Sociological Journal* 1994, no. 2.

natural to certain strata of society that have their own cultural stereotypes and specific patterns of behaviour, both in production activities and in everyday life. Representatives of that subculture live in a cultural environment of their own.

This theory provides a researcher mainly with the means of describing that separate world and helps him identify the factors that should be used to discriminate that culture from the basic one that embraces the majority of population. It emphasises the alienated character of the subculture of poverty and its immunity to the values and norms of the general culture. The theory places emphasis on the conflictual nature of relations between the two cultures and underscores the most important differences between them.

However, interrelations between a subculture and its mother-culture cannot be simply reduced to rejection and conflict, being in fact much more complex. It is supposed that the two cultures nurture each other and are, in fact, dependent on each other.[15]

Research into the mechanisms of such mutual support and mutual reproduction of the two cultures now represents the main task of any study geared towards achieving practical results connected with the formation of an adequate social policy. Purely academic analyses of poverty without a distinct and a well-formulated practical orientation would today be ethically unjustified.

However, it is precisely those points of the above-mentioned theory that weaken it considerably. There is a necessity to find certain theoretical tools that could also help cover the dynamic aspect of poverty. They should provide a researcher and a politician with the proper knowledge and understanding of the mechanisms of reproduction and self-preservation of the main cultural parameters of the phenomenon of poverty.

It should be noted that along with an external resemblance between the 'culture of poverty' in Russia and the corresponding phenomenon in the market economy countries (mostly developing countries, but which did not have a socialist past), the differences between the character of Russian culture and that of those countries are considerable. In the first place, these differences are connected with the fact that the 'culture of poverty', large as it is in those countries, has never been anything more than a subculture, whereas in Russia this 'culture of poverty' originates from the

---

15 This aspect of problem was pointed out by Herbert Gans more than 20 years ago in his work *The Positive Functions of Poverty*. In particular, he says that poverty makes people do some work because they have no other possibilities, thus excluding the non-poor from that work and giving them certain advantages that they would not have otherwise.

basic behavioural patterns that had been characteristic and constituted the foundation of the predominant social system itself. So, strictly speaking, the 'culture of poverty' as it is found in Russia, does not fully conform with the concept of subculture, because a basic culture of well-being and its values is now just being born in Russia.

Precisely for this reason research into the transformation of society as a cultural transition is so very important. Also of special interest are those strategies connected with overcoming poverty. These strategies include restructuring of the most deep-rooted layer of cultural consciousness and transformation of its most conservative and stable components.

In order to achieve that scientific end, we must supplement the above-described theoretical concepts with a socio-economic approach. We agree with Etzioni, who considers that the policy that is being proposed to Russia and that falls within the framework of neo-classical economics, does not directly address problems connected with the transformation of social institutions and changes in culture. These problems can be resolved only by socio-economics, synthesising ideas and results obtained by different social sciences. Within the framework of socio-economics, the transitional period of society is described in terms of a slow and gradual process that can not be accelerated by any artificial incentives. This can be explained by the fact that the culture of the previous period still deeply saturates both the individual and relations within the population as a whole. "Resocialisation of the people can not be hastened".[16]

This position appears to be true, first of all, because of the fact that in Russia mental and behavioural standards and strategies are being formed simultaneously, interacting with the emerging market structures and institutions. They are evolving together, and only those that fit each other the best survive. Without reciprocal support, neither of the components of the new market culture can become an organic part of the social organism.

We consider that the experience we acquired while studying modes of living of the urban population can serve as an extension of the socio-economic approach. This experience gives us grounds to assume that analysis of the problems of the formation of new behavioural strategies taking place in the new conditions, can be done most effectively within the framework of a specific 'production' paradigm.[17]

---

16 Etzioni, Amitai. "How Is Russia Bearing Up?": 37.

17 *Mode of life of a big city population. Tendencies and problems*. Leningrad: Academy of Sciences, 1988: 24-34.

From that point of view, real peculiarities of such concepts as 'mode of life', 'style of life', 'culture of poverty' or 'prosperity' are dictated by the specific sphere of production in which a given social group is active. We shall call this sphere of production 'social production'. External relations of this production with the whole socio-economic system on the macro level on the one hand, and 'interproduction relations' of people with each other in the course of their everyday life on the other, help to reveal the inner logic of the processes (ideal types according to Weber) that ensure stability and reproduction of the corresponding social phenomena. Typical strategies of behaviour are made up from the whole complex of people's actions which allow them most satisfactorily, from their point of view, to preserve and improve their position in the system of those relations. The pursuit of such strategies ensures that degree of successful existence acknowledged by them as a norm. This means that the process of modification of the previously predominant mode of living represents the broadest context within the framework of which research into poverty in modern Russia should be carried out.

At the same time, the theoretical generalisation that any research must have as its basis consists in the fact that the above-mentioned strategy of minimising efforts and all private strategies derived from it cannot be realised today. They are not just ineffective, they simply cannot guarantee survival any more. They cannot guide the lives of the people any more because they are no longer supported by the corresponding paternalistic socialist institutions. This is the principal challenge that the people of Russia face today, and every person has to find his own ways of meeting this challenge.

This does not, however, mean that every strategy of a socialist type has now completely ceased to exist. Having very slim chances of practical realisation, they still continue to dominate people's mentalities, and this will remain the case, unless old stereotypes of behaviour are replaced by new patterns that are more adequate in the changed reality. In our opinion, many types of poverty in Russia come from that innate propensity towards socialist values. Poverty today is not only a result of circumstances; it is no less a result of mental inertia and unpreparedness of the people with regard to other modes of life that they did not know before.

Therefore, in researching strategies that help to overcome poverty (strategies of survival) we reject on principle, just as A. Etzioni did, the behavioural concept according to which a desired and generally approved type of behaviour is an immediate consequence of targeted external stimuli and impacts. The actual process of socio-economic reforms has proved that the same external economic measures provoke different reactions among different social groups. Some of them overcome poverty quickly, whereas others wrestle with a constantly worsening situation.

It is very interesting to observe the process of formation of those strategies where the behaviour of a person is not directly guided by an external stimulus but is rather a result of an internal mental predisposition. In this case, consciousness plays the role of an internal stimulus unaided by any external influence. In any case, of special interest to us are the instances when a person's behaviour is not just a reaction to an adverse social challenge, but is the demonstration of his or her ability to find and make use of new possibilities. In that connection, it is extremely important to single out the two principal types of social challenge as the external stimuli which are a result of the overall transformation of the social situation in Russia.

- The '*negative' stimulus* is connected with the disappearance and abolition of certain socialist institutions and habitual modes of everyday life. It does not offer any options; such a challenge demands an instant reaction, otherwise, survival is impossible.
- The '*positive' stimulus* is connected with the fact that those modes of life which were either unknown or unacceptable and disapproved of in the recent past, have become possible now. In this case, one can either try and avail oneself of the new possibilities, taking the risks of doing so, or renounce them and take no risks at all.

It appears that the timely identification of mental transformations connected with challenges of this type and also identification of the conditions that favour, or, on the contrary, are adverse to those transformations, is of special importance today because it provides possibilities for more adequate social programmes aimed at encouraging active and future-oriented strategies of behaviour. The encouragement of those strategies (and, accordingly, of mental transformations of that kind) is the most important prerequisite for a successful and fast re-forming of society as a whole.

The present epoch of transformation of mentalities and the search for new strategies of survival prompted by it, determines the choice of the object of research that could most vividly illustrate all the complexity and urgency of those transformations. It appears that the poorest strata of the population should serve as such an object, because these social groups are the most vulnerable to the risks connected with the new competitive market economy. One of our leading experts on social security has suggested the following structure of these groups:

- The *deprived categories*, i.e., persons stripped of their social status (alcoholics, mental patients, drug addicts and others) – about 5% of the whole population;
- *People with fixed incomes* (pensioners, families with many children, unmarried mothers and others) – 5-6%;
- The *'new poor'*, i.e., people who have a job but whose salaries are not sufficient for the upkeep of their families – 6-7%.[18]

Research into the modes of life of the above-mentioned categories is, in our opinion, of great significance because the challenges of today are especially topical for these categories. The change of life strategy is the most vital question for them, and so, the strategies that they are working out now and that might eventually become a routine for them, could be called strategies of survival.

There is a supposition, supported by some of our preliminary observations, that behaviour of the representatives of these groups, being a reaction to the situation common to them all, is, nevertheless, considerably different in every group. Explanation of that difference should become an important component of the studies of the strategies aimed at overcoming poverty. There are several hypotheses regarding the possible patterns of behaviour from which the various (but not necessarily poor) strata of society may choose. These hypotheses are in the spirit of Parkinson's system of the correlation of goals and means in human activity. But under the present general transformational shift they can serve only as a starting point for analysis, and that is because models of that kind do not take into account and do not reveal the mental history of this or that choice.

Research into the motives of the 'new poor' when they try to choose the right strategy is naturally of great interest. Today, we have some data on the reaction of those whose social and property status has changed and who have found themselves in the category of the poor after the devaluation of the status of such important institutions as the defence sector and science.[19] Also research on the adaptation of former army officers to civilian life upon being discharged from the Armed Forces (currently undergoing mass reduction), is being finished now.

Such studies cannot yet give a complete and substantial picture of the formation of new strategies through mental shifts, because originally their objective was

---

18 "Say a word for the 'new poor' — Interview with Evgenii Gontmakher, Chairman of the Committee on Social Policy", *Trud* 11 June 1994.

19 Fomin E., I. Osvald and V. Voronkov. *Rüstungsmigration und "brain drain": Zur Situation im militärisch-industriellen Komplex und in den Wissenschafts-Institutionen in Rußland.* Berlin: Berghof-Stiftung für Konfliktforschung, 1993. Arbeits-papier no. 56.

different. Yet the information obtained from them is, in our opinion, quite suitable for a secondary analysis, which could provide answers to the questions raised in the present analysis. In general, surveillance of this category of the poor shows two distinct strategies of their actual behaviour: the passive and the active one.

The *passive strategy* is connected primarily with reacting to the negative aspect of the general socio-economic challenge. It is the reaction to the disappearance of the former social institutions and possibilities connected with them. It is directed at the preservation of the well-being and position reached under the previous socio-economic conditions. This strategy has two variants, the first being a delayed response, leading to a further aggravation of poverty, and the second being a moderately adaptive reaction which can at best ensure preservation of the reached level. Both variants fit quite well, in our opinion, the concept of the 'culture of poverty'.

The *active strategy* is, strictly speaking, a group of strategies representing a reaction to the newly opened opportunities, and thus, they respond to the positive aspect of the general challenge. They fall into the following main categories:

- the *positive career-oriented type*: this is the strategy of upwardly mobile people aiming at entering a more prosperous social stratum. All legal means helping to climb the social ladder are accepted here. The most important consideration is promotion, and therefore all acceptable means are used to achieve it.
- the *positive instrumental type*: this is the strategy of using all newly opened opportunities in the most rational way possible. It is the position of those who want to serve the system using those means and aspiring to those goals that are preferable from the point of view of public interests. Promotion and well-being is a natural and expected (but not sole) motive of social activity in this case.
- the *criminal career-oriented type*: this is the strategy of improving one's living standards through resorting to the means offered by the disorganisation and anomie of contemporary Russian society. The system can be used to one's advantage and even cheated, this being the most effective and direct way to material well-being.

To find out how and under the influence of which factors representatives of the above-indicated risk groups choose their respective strategies is, in our opinion, a problem not only of theoretical but, undoubtedly, of much practical interest.

We can say in this connection that today, for example, changes in the types of behaviour of deprived categories are not exactly predictable. Their position in society has changed profoundly.

On the one hand, society no longer subjects them to repressive means of resocialisation and rehabilitation. Institutions for compulsory treatment of alcoholics and drug addicts have closed down. The articles of the criminal law envisaging different kinds of punishments for so-called 'sponging' (i.e., shirking from work in the public sector) have been abrogated. A person with certain mental disorders can be placed in a special mental institution only by court decision. The understanding that deprived people need first of all every possible kind of social support and social aid has now almost matured, although there are no special programmes, and corresponding institutions are not set up yet. On the other hand, the changed socio-economic situation has made it more difficult for these deprived people to do occasional jobs, and the risk of losing one's permanent place of residence and minimal level of living conditions has also increased.

The most interesting category, from the point of view of mental shifts, is that of destitute people whose deprivation was the result of their personal choice as a specific form of protest against the existing state of things. It is this category of people that might most actively exploit new opportunities. They might even find new strategies that could attain the status of socially successful and socially accepted ones. Yet, at the same time, their choice might be in favour of strategies of a criminal career type.

Analysis of probable behaviour of the poor with fixed incomes (those who live on pensions or who are on welfare) will give a different picture. It can be presumed that a considerable proportion of them will adapt strategies of survival based on paternalistic values, considering that the corresponding state paternalistic institutions are not destroyed, and the principles of their relations with the population remain the same.

For a large part of that category (mostly retired pensioners) the desire to preserve a traditional way of life represents the only strategy of survival. That strategy is determined, in our opinion, by the fact that the new opportunities (positive challenges) offered by market economy do not concern those people.

Both in their own and in the public opinion, this category of people is considered to have fulfilled their social obligations. The advent of such radical social change surprised them at the stage of their life when the vector of their relations with society should have been reversed. Every one of them has fulfilled the demands of the State, now it is time to 'cash the cheque', as was promised by the main socialist principle that 'every citizen receives from public funds his share, which is in an exact proportion to his contribution to the public welfare'.

Poverty among of those people today is the result of the State's default on its payment. Strategies of their behaviour will be shaped through the conflict of two types of mentalities: that of a state employee (creditor) against that of the State (debtor). These are strategies of mutual compromises, and the final outcome will depend not on the mutual commitments regarding property issues but on the political situation of the moment. Such a conflict has no perspective with regard to its capacity to engender new market strategies. This type of poverty and stereotypes corresponding to it will disappear only with their bearers. They have no future outside traditional modes of life, and thus the struggle to return to the former conditions is in this case a struggle for survival.

Because of the lack of special studies, poverty in Russia today is a subject of political speculations of all kinds. Politicians are concerned in the first instance with social tension: as soon as poverty reaches the degree at which a social outbreak becomes possible, the State will inevitably have to change the present course of reforms in favour of more populist strategies.

We have sufficient grounds to state that poverty in Russia does not have a universal character, as is widely believed. Moreover, the probability of social outbreak in this connection is most unlikely. The market offers everybody immense opportunities, and the speed and scale of transformation of 'Soviet' mentalities should not be underestimated either.

The population of Russia is adapting fairly rapidly to the new conditions and is finding effective strategies of a new economic behaviour. Meanwhile, those who cannot for different reasons do anything to change their life, generally belong to the groups incapable of active social protest.

The answer 'yes' to a question typical in public surveys, namely "Will you take part in meetings or demonstrations of protest against growing prices and a fall in living standards?" (this number oscillates between 20-25%)[20] cannot be interpreted monosemantically, just as the majority of answers in such surveys cannot be. In reality, it is practically impossible to observe any actions of protest in connection with poverty.

---

20 "Economic and Social Changes: Monitoring Public Opinion." *Informational Bulletin* 1994, no. 6: 47.

Universal poverty in Russia has become a truism in the public consciousness, but is it so in reality? We would like to say some words in this connection.

1. The idea of poverty among the Russian people is formed by the mass media and differs considerably from the opinion held by the population itself, especially in those cases where people can compare their own experience with information given in the mass media. This is indirectly illustrated by the results of the surveys conducted by the Russian *Centre of Public Opinion Studies*, in which the economic situation in Russia is characterised as 'bad' or 'very bad' (65%) whereas the economic situation in the town or countryside district of a respondent is assessed as 'bad' by only 50% of the respondents. This discrepancy is even more pronounced in the case of assessment of the economic situation of the family of a respondent (40%).[21] The majority of our interviews confirm the belief of respondents that almost the entire Russian population lives in absolute misery, and here a respondent usually adds "my family is, thank God, an exception, we have managed to overcome our difficulties".
2. The 'culture of poverty', a prevailing one up to the present moment, has taught people to pretend to be poorer than they actually are. The majority of the respondents considered themselves to be poor, even if they had absolutely no reasons for saying so.

   However, many of them were quite sincere in saying that they feel that they are poor despite the fact that their living standards have risen over these last years. This is connected with the fact that differences in living standards were inconspicuous in the past; theoretically, everyone could buy any object displayed in the shops (but because of the acute deficit the choice was very limited). Now, however, there are a great number of things, absolutely unaffordable to ordinary consumers, and their resentfulness is aggravated by an ostentatious display of the luxuriant lifestyles of the *nouveaux riches*. Under the present circumstances people compare their possibilities with possibilities of the categories with the highest incomes, and that makes them feel their own relative deprivation and poverty.

   The high proportion of people claiming their impoverishment in public opinion polls is connected with a psychological aspect of poverty and is not confirmed by calculations of incomes of any kind.

21 Ibidem: 46.

3. No expert and no calculations can identify, even approximately, the actual income level in different social groups. It can be positively presumed that the better part of the incomes of the population is not registered in any way since it is obtained in the informal sector of the economy that is so extraordinarily developed in Russia today.[22]

   We cannot rely on statistics, the credibility of which has always been questioned. Today, now that the social institution of statistics is crumbling, it cannot serve as a basis for the analysis of any process under the present period of rapid social changes.

   Mass questionnaires, which are still being overestimated by Russian sociologists, only strengthen the myth of general poverty, as their results with regard to such a delicate theme as incomes, are highly doubtful. People conceal their informal incomes, fearing both tax collectors and racketeers and simply to be 'on the safe side', because of irrational and unspecified fears so characteristic of a Soviet person in the past.

   Our own research was based on deep probe interviewing, in which we questioned people who trusted us and could speak frankly about their illegal activities and illegal incomes. The very possibility of research giving the real picture of income groups is seriously doubtful – the great majority of our respondents did have officially unregistered incomes, the size of which was considerably greater than that of their declared incomes (in some cases dozens of times bigger!).

   Interviews demonstrated one more paradox in the consciousness of Russians, the effect of which is not taken into account in studies based on other methods. The great majority of people talking about income mean only regularly received money income (salary, pension, etc.), and do not even mention occasional earnings (especially earnings in hard currency), to say nothing of non-money incomes (in the form of agricultural products from their plots of land).
4. Under the current rapid economic and social changes, the economic status of a person changes frequently, the level of material well-being jumps and falls sharply. Under these conditions it is especially easy to note that the proportion of those who are constantly poor is relatively small. For the majority of people,

---

22 An indirect proof to this statement is an estimate of situation in Uzbekistan. In 1993 official money income amounted there to 308.8 mld roubles, whereas personal hidden income amounted to 2,179.6 mld roubles! Experts note that illegal incomes grow faster. (Ongov, U. "Majority of Population Lives on Unearned Income." *Segodnya* 7 April 1994).

poverty is a temporary difficulty to be quickly overcome, and in every particular case we observe, what can be termed a 'career of poverty'.

In this connection, an important psychological effect should be noted, namely a delayed realisation of one's actual economic status and level of well-being, a realisation which follows changes with a certain lag. People who have essentially improved their material situation continue to feel emotions reflecting their previous poor conditions and say, as they did before, that they are poor.

5. It is clear that several percent of the population are constantly poor and have no chance of changing this situation on their own. It is, of course, a task of society to provide them with human living conditions. Nevertheless, in this category of respondents the percentage of those completely socialised in the 'culture of poverty', and for this reason content with their miserable situation, is especially high. This phenomenon was also noted in our studies conducted during the period of 'developed socialism'.
6. Finally, neither researchers nor the people realise the peculiar feature of Russian society that makes it impossible to compare the scale and nature of poverty in Russia with that of other countries. This is the fact that as a result of the free privatisation of apartments almost everyone now possesses real and rather considerable assets. Taking into consideration that a very large part of population own small plots of land and a second dwelling (dacha), we begin to understand that we know very little about poverty in Russia. Future research promises a great number of unexpected discoveries.

3

Social and Geographical Analysis of the Flow and Territorial Distribution of Refugees and Migrants in Russia

Vladimir Kozlov

Forced migration, the major component of which is the flow of refugees and migrants which has grown considerably during the past few years, is a complex phenomenon possessing different aspects: political, legal, economic, social, psychological, ecological, etc. This article presents an analysis of the social and geographical aspects of this phenomenon, i.e., the dynamics of the flow of refugees and migrants (resettlers) from the CIS countries and the Baltic states to Russia; their distribution across Russian regions; the main regional problems connected with their arrival in Russia, and the state policy for their settlement.

The Problem of Forced Migrants in Russia.

Forced migration is migration under the influence or threat of the use of force or, as analysts say, migration which is not connected with positive motivation or attractive opportunities in new places[1]. Forced migration has become rather typical for Russian history. In the Soviet period it took place in a wide variety of different forms, giving rise to mass movements of population either outside or within the country.

The most massive resettlements of people within Russia and the Soviet Union were during the disfranchisement of the *kulaks*; during the struggle with the 'enemies of the people' and creation of the *gulag*, evacuations during the Second World War, deportation of the peoples and 'selective exile' in the post-war period.

To some degree, these movements of people may also be called forced migration: resettlements connected with rendering 'friendly help' to the ethnic republics in building up their industry, science and education; development of the *virgin lands*;

---

1 Vitkovskaya, G.S. *Vynuzhdennaya migratsiya: problemy i perspektivy* [Forced Migration: Problems and Perspectives]. Vol. 3. Institute of Forecasts in the National Economy. Moscow: Russian Academy of Sciences, 1993.

Komsomol and five-year plan construction projects which continued until the 1980s. Forced migrants in each of the mentioned cases were counted by hundreds of thousands and sometimes by millions. In terms of time, these deportations were either extended for many years or completed very quickly in several days.

Though the term 'refugees' started to be used after the First World War, in the USSR it was not widely applied. Of course, there were refugees here before, i.e., refugees who were trying to escape from German and Spanish fascism, and those who were evacuated during the war, but all these events were connected with external factors. Until the 1980s the term 'refugees' was used only with reference to the events in Palestine, Vietnam, Ethiopia, Afghanistan and other countries suffering from wars and natural disasters. Some of these refugees received political asylum, employment and education in the USSR, but, in general, the problem of the refugees did not exist in the USSR because there were very few of them and the state rendered all the necessary financial and material support to them. They were usually placed in the capital or in capitals of the regions ('*oblast'* centres').

Only in the late 1980s, when the victims of *pogroms* in Azerbaidzhan and Uzbekistan rushed to Moscow and the North Caucasus, did people in Russia start talking about the refugees, whose migration was caused by 'local factors'.

However, an understanding that this phenomenon is a massive one came late. The history of internal refugees in Russia has deep roots. Analysts point out different reasons for such massive movements of refugees to have started in the post-war years. However, most experts agree that contemporary migration processes were connected with the exodus of ethnic Russians from the FSU republics in the early 1970s – first from the Trans-Caucasian republics and later on from Central Asia[2].

Statistics show that by the mid-1970s Russia kept losing population due to migration, but after that the population started to grow for the same reason. Thus, radical changes in the inter-republican migration vector had happened long before inter-ethnic relations became aggravated. The first reason for that was economic decline and the increase in the use of 'ethnic principles' in social welfare distribution in most of the Soviet Union republics which led to the 'soft' driving out of Russian-speakers, and above all, of ethnic Russians from these republics. This all took place in a relatively calm atmosphere within the boundaries of a 'unified' common state. Therefore, nobody used to call migrants who were coming to Russia from ethnic

---

2 Perevedentsev, V.I. *Raspad SSSR i problemy repatriatsii v Rossiyu* [The Breakup of the USSR and the Problems of Repatriation to Russia]. "Refugees" Russian Independent Institute of Social and National Problems. Moscow, 1993.

republics either 'refugees' or 'forced migrants', though most of them were such *de facto*.

People who worked at the so-called 'construction projects of Communism' may also be called refugees of this type, because analysis of the motives for coming to such projects shows that material interests were secondary reasons for moving, and likewise it is not attributable to any attempts to improve living conditions. The forced nature of migration was hidden under the ideological slogans of being 'economic missionaries'[3].

Today the term 'refugees' is often applied to all migrants that continue to arrive in Russia. This is not correct for several reasons.

Firstly, 'refugees' make up only a part of all forced migrants, whose numbers also include people who have suffered from ecological disasters; military servicemen left unemployed and homeless as a result of the withdrawal of troops from other countries, nations that had suffered repressions and are returning to their native land, etc.

Secondly, most of our 'refugees' were and are still not recognised as such *de iure*. Refugee status according to international law and the Russian law *On refugees* (passed in March, 1993) may be granted to foreign citizens only. Therefore, before the break-up of the USSR there could be no refugees 'by definition'. Even now, bearing in mind that it is comparatively easy for former residents of the USSR to acquire Russian citizenship, not too much importance should be attributed to the fact whether a former Soviet citizen has Russian citizenship or not. If only formal definitions were observed, the problem of refugees could be easily 'solved' by granting citizenship. However, formal acquisition of Russian citizenship does not solve the problem of 'forced migration' and the acceptance of compatriots in Russia.

Further on we shall discuss the problem of forced migrants from the FSU countries including both refugees and resettlers in this group because they used to be registered together. Nowadays it is difficult to formally distinguish between them, however, this difference is rather unimportant for social and geographical analysis.

2 The Number of Real and Potential Migrants and Refugees

No one knows how many refugees and migrants there are in Russia now. This problem is connected with restrictions in registration (i.e., with the *propiska* –

---

3 Sheregi, F.I. *K voprosu ob istokakh problemy 'Bezhentsy'* [On the Origin of the Problem of 'Refugees']. Moscow: Russian Independent Institute of Social and National Problems, 1993.

registration of any resident with the militia) and unwillingness of some migrants to be registered at all because such registration grants them no particular privileges.

According to the latest official data of the Federal Migration Service of Russia (FMS) over 640,000 refugees and forced migrants have already been registered. However, this service registers only migrants who satisfy the requirements stipulated by the laws *On Refugees* and *On Forced Migrants*. It is perfectly clear that the real number is higher. Even the director of the FMS has spoken of 500,000 refugees, 1 million forced migrants and 500,000 'economic' migrants[4].

Some estimates mention 4 million forced migrants, though the methods of calculation are unclear. Reports of the number of forced migrants in separate cities and regions also differ. Official and unofficial reports of the number of refugees and migrants differ substantially for the cities and regions with restricted *propiska*– primarily Moscow and Krasnodar *krai*. Officially, slightly over 15,000 people have been registered in each, but according to unofficial estimates the real figure approaches half a million migrants in both cases.

However, it should be remembered that such 'maximalist' estimates usually include data on all categories of legal and illegal migrants, not only from CIS countries and Baltic states, but from countries of the 'far abroad', such as Somalia, Ethiopia, Afghanistan (these were not registered by the FMS for a long time), as well as economic migrants.

Another considerable problem is the potential number of forced migrants – those who intend to move to Russia. Here it is important to know not only how many people are willing to immigrate, but also when they are going to come. There is no universal approach to this problem. There exist two extreme points of view. Journalists and politicians more often display 'alarmist' and extremist views. They proceed from assessments of the situation as being 'catastrophic' and forecast a rapid increase of the inflow of refugees in the near future. Sociologists and demographers, on the other hand, display a more balanced approach as they believe that this process may be compared in its scale to migration in the recent past and that one should not expect an 'avalanche' of millions of refugees into Russia in the next few years. However, similarity in the scale of these events does not mean similarity in their essence. It is one thing when movement is planned and performed in a calm atmosphere under conditions of comparatively equal exchange of flats, a common 'rouble zone', etc., and quite another when the movement is sudden, caused by the

4 *Problems of Refugees and Forced Migrants*. Moscow: Proceedings of an International Conference. International Association of the Peace Foundation, 1994.

threat of violence. Differences in these two approaches concern not only the numbers of potential migrants but also the terms of their coming to Russia. The last census in Russia was held in 1989. According to this census, 25.3 million Russians and slightly over 3 million people whose ethnic territories are in Russia (Tatars, Bashkirs, Mordvians, etc.) were living outside Russia. In the intervening years their numbers are unlikely to have increased because Russians are not characterised by high levels of population growth in 'peaceful years', and some of them have already moved to Russia. Nevertheless, higher estimates reaching figures of up to 38 million (25 million Russians and 11 million people who are ethnically, historically and culturally of Russian heritage) appear in the press. The number of potential migrants mentioned by the newspapers was never below 25 million Russians (28 million including such nationalities as mentioned above), however 2 and even 4 million refugees and forced migrants have been mentioned alongside those who had already immigrated to Russia. Perhaps this is an artificial aggravation of the situation. There is no reason to talk about the return of 25 million Russians to their historical motherland because most of them live in comparatively calm regions i.e., in Ukraine and Belarus, where more Russians had been coming to live in recent years than were actually leaving.

According to the specialist's forecasts prepared for the new federal migration programme, the inflow of refugees and migrants into Russia from the CIS countries and the Baltic states may be estimated at at least 800,000 in 1994-1996, the average number of those looking for asylum, at least 2-3 million and at most 4 to 6 million people. The FMS itself is set to receive 400,000 refugees and migrants annually.

However, today this forecast is being interpreted in a different way. Some analysts say that 'over two years it is necessary to expect 6 million refugees', while other suggest that only average estimates should be considered because the mentioned numbers are likely to be reached only by 2005. It is easy to calculate that these estimates differ in terms of the exponent: from 300,000 to 3 million refugees and migrants per annum. It is evident that the reason for choosing maximal estimates is purely political.

Further on we shall refer to the official FMS reports of the registration of refugees and forced migrants because this data allows to produce a social and geographical analysis of the problem. It should also be noted that in individual, mainly frontier regions official figures have been lowered.

3 Dynamics of the Flow of Refugees into Russia and Territories from Which Refugees Flee to Russia

As has been mentioned above, the flow of refugees and migrants sharply increased in the late 1980s. The first wave of migrants into Russia occurred in 1988 after the events in Baku and Sumgait when the city of Moscow and Moscow *oblast'* alone received about 55,000 refugees, mainly Russians and Armenians. In 1989 over 60,000 Meshketian Turks were forced to move from Fergana. Most of them were settled in six Central Russian *oblasts*, including Smolensk, Belgorod and Voronezh *oblasts*. Following this Russia received 10,000 Chechens from Kazakhstan. When the Karabakh war began in 1990, refugees started moving by hundreds of thousands not only into the conflicting republics, but also into central Russia and Russian regions of the Caucasus – Krasnodar and Stavropol' *krais* and Rostov *oblast'*. In 1991 Ossetian refugees from South Ossetia and inner regions of Georgia joined this flow. Practically all Ossetians (80,000 were registered but their actual number is estimated at over 100,000) settled in North Ossetia where they have so far remained.

After the break-up of the USSR the flow of migrants increased significantly. This was caused by the aggravation of the political situation, economic crisis, laws on languages and citizenship discriminating against the non-natives, everyday nationalism, and growth of intolerance leading to inter-ethnic conflicts in the FSU republics. It is worth mentioning that tension and clashes in the FSU republics and in some regions of Russia were caused not only by inter-ethnic relations and conflicts of an ethnic and cultural nature based upon the 'polarity' of Christian and Muslim cultures, as is often the explanation. For instance, in Tadzhikistan the conflict is of a subethnic nature involving people of one nationality but belonging to different clans. There are numerous examples of violent clashes between the representatives of one confession (either Christian or Muslim), such as clashes between Georgians and Ossetians, Kazakhs and Chechens, or the deportation of the Meskhetian Turks.

In 1992 the Dnestr region, Tadzhikistan, Abkhasia and North Ossetia (the Ingush were leaving the Prigorodnyi district of this region) joined the regions from which refugees were fleeing.

In June 1992 the Federal Migration Service of Russia was set up and official registration of refugees (forced migrants) began, although there was no corresponding Russian legislation at that time. At the initial stage only those who were coming from the regions of military conflicts (such as Azerbaidzhan, Moldova, Georgia, Tadzhikistan and Chechnya) could claim refugee status. Later on, residents

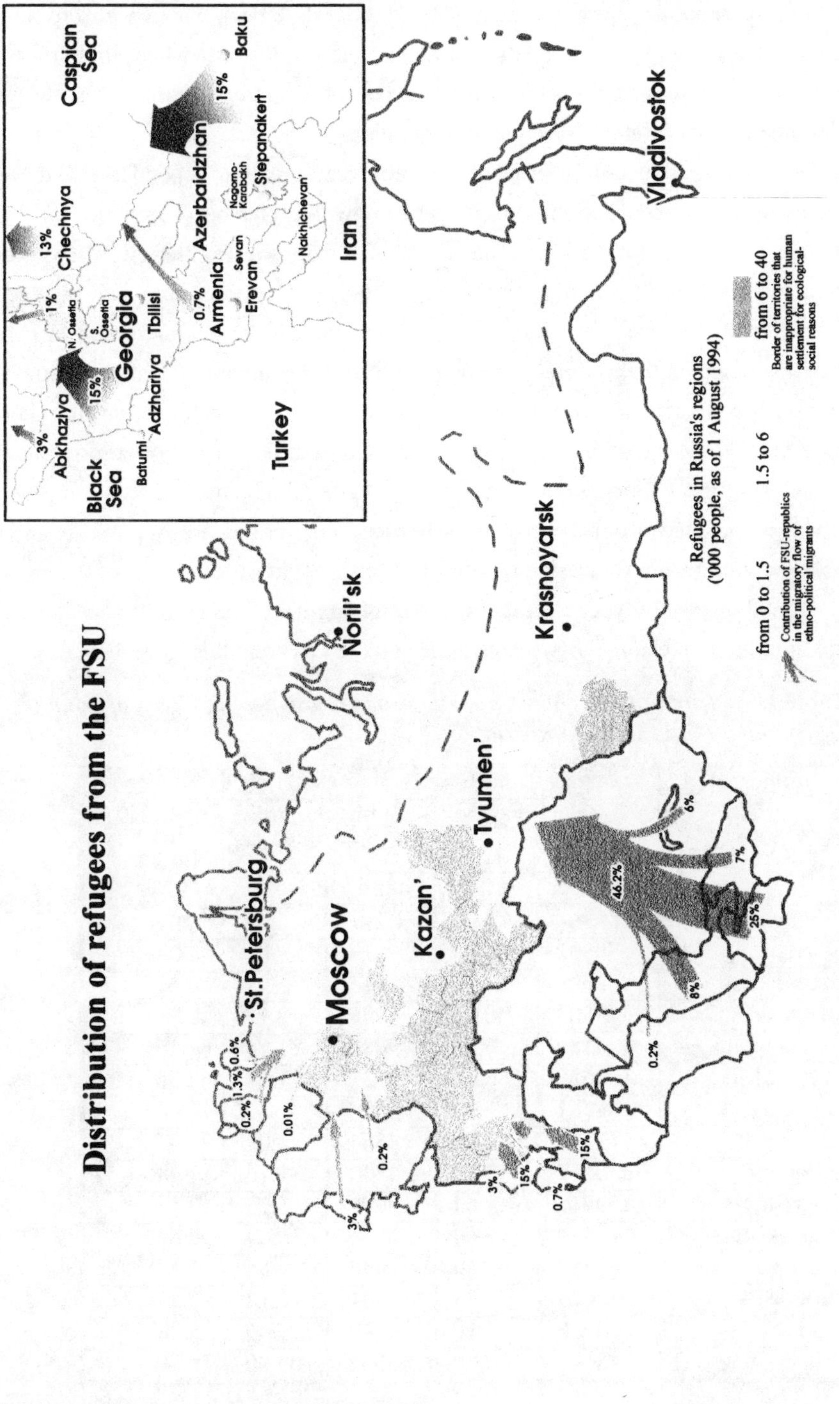
Distribution of refugees from the FSU
St.Petersburg
Moscow
Kazan'
Tyumen'
Noril'sk
Krasnoyarsk
Vladivostok
Black Sea
Caspian Sea
Abkhaziya
Adzhariya
Batumi
Georgia
Tbilisi
N. Osetia
S. Osetia
Chechnya
Armenia
Erevan
Sevan
Azerbaidzhan
Nagorno-Karabakh
Stepanakert
Nakhichevan'
Baku
Turkey
Iran
3%
15%
1%
13%
0.7%
15%
0.2%
1.3%
0.6%
0.01%
0.2%
3%
3%
15%
0.7%
15%
0.2%
8%
46.2%
25%
7%
6%
Refugees in Russia's regions
('000 people, as of 1 August 1994)
from 0 to 1.5
1.5 to 6
from 6 to 40
Contribution of FSU-republics in the migratory flow of ethno-political migrants
Border of territories that are inappropriate for human settlement for ecological-social reasons

of all FSU republics started to be registered, but while people arriving from the first group of regions were practically always granted this status when applying to the FMS, only approximately 40% of newcomers from relatively calm areas (Armenia, Turkmenia and Ukraine) were granted this status.

Granting the status of 'a refugee' or of a 'forced migrant' depended also upon the region in which people applied for it. In Moscow, St.Petersburg and practically in all *oblast'* capitals as well as in some *oblasts* far from the frontier (were there are a great number of forced migrants) these people were registered and granted the desired status only if they had close relatives resident there who agreed to register the newcomers at their homes. The number of *oblasts* in which local authorities pass decisions on 'temporary' measures of migration control (in practice, on strict control over the admittance of migrants) is growing constantly. This is often done in clear violation of the Constitution of the Russian Federation. Thus, in Kostroma *oblast'* which is far away from the country's borders, restrictions are imposed even upon people coming from Caucasian republics which are part of Russia.

Over the last few years, refugees and migrants have contributed substantially to the 'migration exchange' between Russia and the FSU republics (see Table 1).

Table 1 *Contribution of refugees and migrants to the flow of migrants from the CIS and Baltic states to Russia.*

Region of Origin	Arrivals in Russia (1992-1993)				% of R&Rs among Migrants
	Total Migrants		Refugees and Resettlers (R&Rs)		
	Number	%	Number	%	
Ukraine	388764	21.03	281	.08	.07
Belarus	70902	3.84	17	.00	.02
Uzbekistan	203606	11.01	21613	5.91	10.62
Kazakhstan	379563	20.53	7948	2.17	2.09
Georgia	124181	6.72	79682	21.78	64.17
Azerbaidzhan	124627	6.74	77339	21.14	62.06
Lithuania	34761	1.88	509	.14	1.46
Moldova	51684	2.80	14664	4.01	28.37
Latvia	53162	2.88	4240	1.16	7.98
Kirgizstan	159711	8.64	20971	5.73	13.13
Tadzhikistan	141319	7.64	134046	36.64	94.85
Armenia	45556	2.46	1990	.54	4.37
Turkmenistan	32025	1.73	504	.14	1.57
Estonia	38780	2.10	2048	.56	5.28
Total	1848641	100.00	365852	100.00	19.79

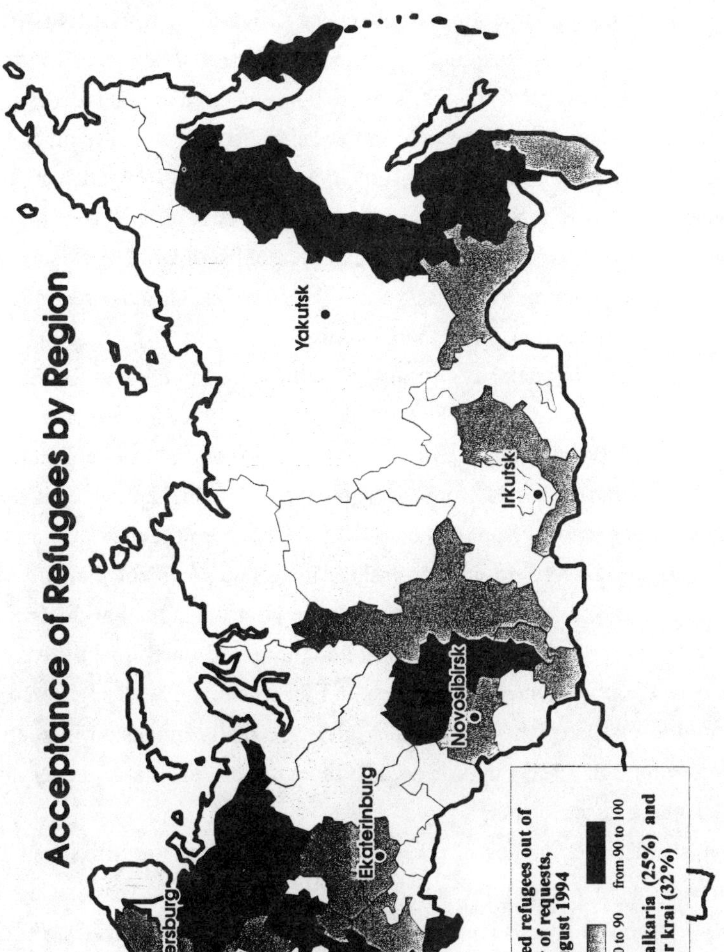
Acceptance of Refugees by Region
Yakutsk
Irkutsk
Novosibirsk
Ekaterinburg
St.Petersburg
Moscow
Rostov-on-the-Don
Vladikavkaz
Number of accepted refugees out of total number of requests, % on 1 August 1994
from 25 to 80
from 80 to 90
from 90 to 100
min- Kabardino-Balkaria (25%) and Krasnodar krai (32%)

One can see from the table that almost every fifth person who arrived in Russia in 1992-1993 is either an officially registered refugee or a forced migrant. Their number is slightly bigger if those who were not registered are included.

The greatest share of refugees and forced migrants in the total number of migrants is typical for Tadzhikistan (almost 100%), Georgia and Azerbaidzhan (over 60%). The table also shows that the total number of migrants differs from the number of forced migrants. Thus, the share of Ukraine, Kazakhstan and Uzbekistan in the total flow of migrants coming into Russia was over 50% (for all those republics) while in the case of forced migrants their share is only 8%.

The overwhelming majority of refugees and forced migrants to Russia come from the FSU republics in which inter-ethnic conflicts followed by armed clashes are (or were) going on. By 1 August 1994 a quarter of all reported refugees came to Russia from Tadzhikistan and 15% from Georgia and Azerbaidzhan respectively. Another 12% of refugees arrived from Chechnya. If we compare the data available for those states where there were no armed clashes, it becomes evident that the majority of refugees come not from the places where state policy is aimed at driving out ethnic Russians or where there are legal restrictions imposed on Russian-speakers (as, for instance, in Latvia or Estonia which account for less than 2% of registered refugees), but from those places where political leaders are really interested in keeping ethnic Russians, although discrimination against them on the regional and everyday level is high (Kirghizia, Kazakhstan).

Analysis of the dynamics of refugee and migrant flow into Russia shows that its structure varies, depending on the situation in the republics. While at the beginning of 1994 forced migrants from regions featuring armed clashes (Tadzhikistan, Georgia, Azerbaidzhan, Chechnya) comprised about 80% of the total flow, the data obtained for seven months of 1994 show that the situation has changed dramatically (see Table 2). The share of the mentioned regions has decreased to one-third and the majority of refugees and migrants were arriving from Kazakhstan, Uzbekistan (20% respectively) and Kirghizia (16%), i.e., states where discrimination is high at local levels.

Table 2 *The flow of refugees and migrants into Russia*

Region of Origin	Number and Percentage (in % of Total Number) of Refugees and Resettlers, arrived in Russia					
	on 1 January 1994		Jan – Aug 1994		On 1 August 1994	
	Number	%	Number	%	Number	%
Moldova	14664	3.27	1577	1.27	16241	2.84
Azerbaidzhan	77339	17.27	7848	6.31	85187	14.88
Georgia	79682	17.79	9009	7.24	88691	15.50
Abkhasia	11198	2.50	2489	2.00	13687	2.39
Tadzhikistan	134046	29.93	11872	9.54	145918	25.50
Chechnya	59972	13.39	13099	10.53	73071	12.77
Ingushetia	2273	.51	92	.07	2365	.41
Kazakhstan	7948	1.77	24256	19.50	32204	5.63
Uzbekistan	21613	4.83	24515	19.71	46128	8.06
Latvia	4240	.95	2932	2.36	7172	1.25
Lithuania	509	.11	610	.49	1119	.20
Estonia	2048	.46	1424	1.14	3472	.61
Armenia	1990	.44	2188	1.76	4178	.73
Ukraine	281	.06	946	.76	1227	.21
Kirghizia	20971	4.68	20258	16.28	41229	7.20
Turkmenistan	504	.11	588	.47	1092	.19
Belarus	17	.00	39	.03	56	.01
Russia	1826	.41	162	.13	1988	.35
Ossetia	5880	1.31	343	.28	6223	1.09
Other	932	.21	155	.12	1087	.19
Total	447933	100.00	124402	100.00	572335	100.00

Another tendency that marks changes in the flow of migrants is that this flow becomes russified. While the first groups of forced migrants coming to Russia consisted mainly of Armenians, Azerbaidzhani, Meskhetian Turks and Ossetians, starting from 1992 the majority of them consisted of Russians. Today the share of Russians is estimated at more than 60%, of Ossetians, Armenians and Tatars – at 7-9% each, Ukrainians – 3%, Georgians and Tadzhiks – slightly over 1%. Latest reports confirm this tendency. Today, ethnic Russians make up 63% of refugees and 75% of forced migrants.

Recently the flow of refugees and forced migrants has, according to official statistics, somewhat reduced. While in 1993 it was estimated at an average of 23,800 a month, for the first seven months of 1994 the average figure was 17,800 people. This may be explained by several reasons pertaining to the situation in the FSU republics and in Russia. In that same year inter-ethnic and armed clashes became less intensive and the policy of local authorities towards the Russian-speaking population became more balanced. Migration potential in some of the republics (Armenia, Azerbaidzhan, Georgia, Tadzhikistan) has been practically exhausted – all Russians that wanted to leave have already done so. The declarations and laws aimed at supporting Russians abroad, which have lately started to appear, also contributed to keeping Russians in the places of their residence. The long-term effect of this factor will depend upon the practical implementation of these promises.

Another factor that caused a reduction of the flow of refugees is the way in which Russia accepts refugees and migrants. Lack of care, real assistance and support (above all, lack of financial aid), endless problems connected with settling and employment force potential migrants to stay in even the most volatile places. Many instances of migrants returning from Russia to their places of residence have been registered: several thousand Russians returned to relatively calm Kirgizstan and even to Tadzhikistan where tension is extremely high.

However, a certain reduction of the flow of refugees does not provide grounds for making predictions about the future. Any aggravation of inter-ethnic relations, infringement of the rights of Russians and other non-native nations may provoke another massive wave of forced migrants fleeing to Russia. The situation in Kazakhstan is especially worrying, because the number of ethnic Russians living there is significant but the policy of the administration, especially local, is aimed at infringement of their rights and freedoms. This factor has increased tension in inter-ethnic relations and the declarations of certain Russian political and public leaders only make it worse.

4 Geography and Factors of Distribution of Refugees and Migrants in the Regions of Russia

Refugees and migrants have already spread across the whole territory of Russia, except regions of the Far North and several ethnic republics such as Yakutia, Chechnya and Adygeya. The main areas of their settling are the North Caucasus, the southern frontier regions of the black-earth zone, the Volga region and the Urals. Most of them are concentrated in North Ossetia and territories adjacent to southern republics – Stavropol' *krai*, Belgorod, Rostov, Orenburg, Voronezh, Saratov and Volgograd *oblasts* and in Krasnodar *krai*. The majority of the forced migrants are concentrated in the cities. In northern and eastern regions about 100% of all migrants settle in cities, while in southern regions of central Russia, the North Caucasus, Urals and Western Siberia they prefer to stay in the countryside.

The distribution of forced migrants over Russia was spontaneous because there were no state programmes for their distribution in the country. The place of residence was usually chosen by the migrants with regard to the distance factor (whether it was easier and cheaper to move to the adjacent region), desire to live closer to the place of former residence in similar geographical and climatic conditions, or whether there were relatives or friends living there.

For these reasons refugees from Tadzhikistan usually settle in the ethnic Russian territories adjacent to their republics, mainly along the railway running from Tadzhikistan to central Russia, and also in the southern Urals, the central Volga regions and in south-central Russia. Refugees from Azerbaidzhan mainly prefer to settle in Stavropol' *krai*, Saratov, Samara and Belgorod *oblasts*. The majority of refugees from Chechnya settle in the ethnic Russian North Caucasus, Belgorod and Voronezh *oblasts*. Almost half of the refugees from Georgia (mainly Ossetians from South Ossetia and inner Georgia) have settled in North Ossetia. Refugees of other nationalities mainly concentrate in the ethnic Russian regions of the North Caucasus.

National and cultural factors are important when deciding where to settle. Refugees try to return to their historical motherland, to re-unite with their relatives and rely not only upon state aid but also on the support of the local national public organisations.

Thus, Russian refugees very seldom settle in the ethnic republics (e.g. in Tatarstan, Dagestan, Tuva and North Ossetia) where their share in the total number of refugees is less than 10%. At the *oblast'* level, the smallest share of Russian refugees is registered in Orenburg *oblast'* (57%), where many Tatars and Bashkirs live, and in Kaliningrad *oblast'* (45%). Armenian refugees, most of whom came not from Armenia but from Azerbaidzhan, Nagorno-Karabakh and Abkhazia, are concentrated in the North Caucasus and in Saratov *oblast'*. Great numbers of Armenian refugees have been registered in big cities, especially in Moscow (58%) and in Kaliningrad *oblast'*.

Refugees of Islamic heritage (Tatars, Bashkirs, Tadzhiks, Uzbeks, Kirghiz, and others, with the exception of Azerbaidzhanis) prefer to settle in Tatarstan and Bashkiria or in the adjacent Volga and Urals regions where the Tatar population is high.

Practically all refugees of nationalities that have their autonomies in the Russian Federation settle in the corresponding republics (Komi, Karel, Chuvash, etc.)

Each of the nations is characterised by certain migratory behaviour reflected in the choice of the region in Russia, and in their expectations. Some nationalities (ethnic Russians, Tatars, etc., who have their national and state formations) come to settle for life in the new place, while Chechens and some other refugees mostly intend to go back when the situation becomes stable (the so-called 'migrant-returnees'). The third group intends to emigrate to other countries, treating Russia merely as a place where they can wait for permission to emigrate; among this group there are numbers of Armenians, Germans, Greeks and Jews and practically all refugees from 'the far abroad' (the so-called 'transit migrants').

Undoubtedly, the process of organised re-settlement of the refugees, which the State is trying to achieve and which has been outlined by the federal migration programme, has to consider all tendencies of their spontaneous distribution in Russia, since it seems unrealistic to change these tendencies, especially in today's conditions of economic and political crisis. Therefore, only certain corrections may be introduced into this process. Further on, we shall discuss how these tendencies are considered by the state policy.

5 Influence of the Refugees on the Demographic, Social, Economic and Political Situation

The influence of the refugees and migrants upon the general situation in Russia can be assessed from different points of view. In view of the decrease in the population which began in 1992, decreasing life expectancy, depopulation of rural areas, the inflow is a positive factor that contributes to the replenishment of the demographic and economic potential of the country with the help of the refugees and migrants, most of whom are educated and highly qualified specialists.

However, unfortunately, this is only a theoretical reasoning. In real life and in the conditions of modern Russia the inflow of migrants is recognised as an 'interfering factor'. It is considered that refugees and migrants give rise to a great number of problems, which are aggravated by the economic crisis, low living standards, growing unemployment, inadequate financing of migration programmes by the State, imperfect legislation and the 'overlap' of several migration flows. Thus in 1990-1992, 270,000 people migrated from the northern territories to central Russia, the North Caucasus and the Volga region (i.e., to the regions where the main bulk of refugees is concentrated).

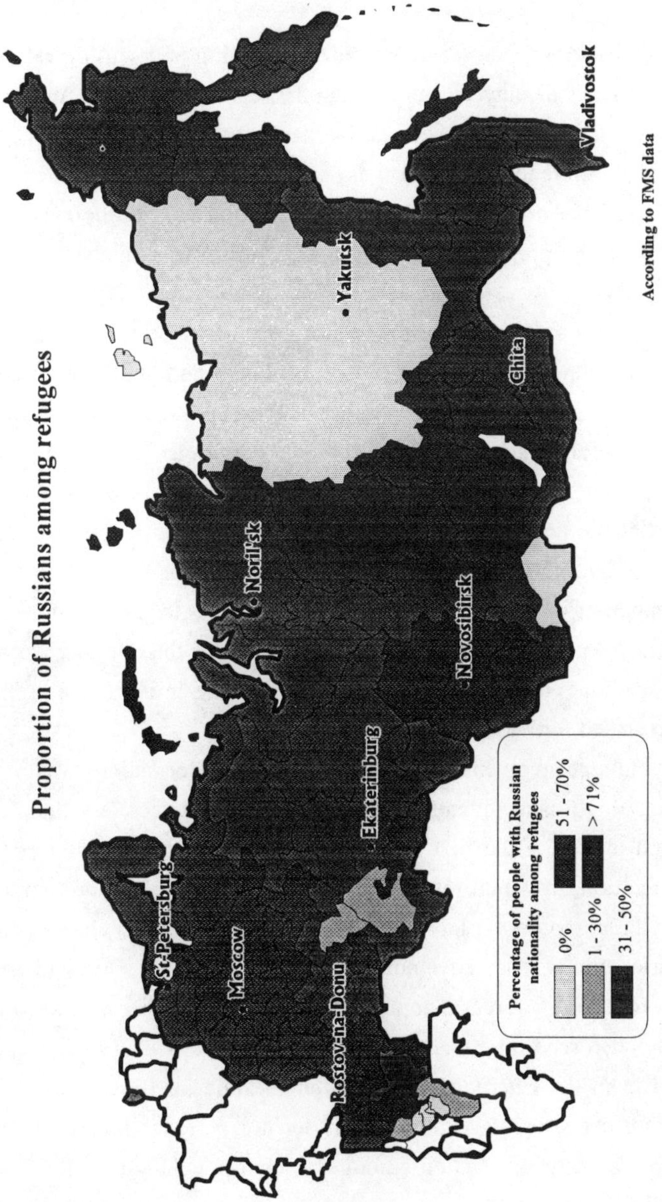
Proportion of Russians among refugees
St-Petersburg
Moscow
Rostov-na-Donu
Ekaterinburg
Noril'sk
Novosibirsk
Yakutsk
Chita
Vladivostok
Percentage of people with Russian nationality among refugees
0%
1 - 30%
31 - 50%
51 - 70%
>71%
According to FMS data

The fact that the State is not interested in receiving and settling refugees in the Russian territories is displayed both through the reduction of funds allocated for this purpose, which are marked in the state budget as 'miscellaneous costs', and in the state policy with reference to compatriots, which is aimed at keeping Russians in the FSU republics. This policy is being openly attributed to economic and political reasons, because the presence of a *diaspora* in any other country is an important factor of influence.

Refugees and migrants also feel the indifference of the State. They left for Russia in the hope of putting into practice their knowledge and skills, but received only sympathy and feigned assistance at best. Certainly, there were some positive examples, but unfortunately they were not very numerous, and besides, after some period of hopes and initial success, disappointment frequently set in. Therefore, it is quite clear that the majority of refugees and migrants are people dissatisfied with their position, blaming the Russian authorities for all their troubles, unhappy about all that is happening in Russia, often having no resources to survive in their places of residence. They represent a potential social resource for the criminal world, starting from small speculation and parasitism and culminating in participation in criminal business and armed formations.

Direct or indirect involvement of refugees in armed formations was registered in the Sumgait and Dushanbe events and in the conflicts between Ossetians and Ingush in the autumn of 1992 – the first bloody inter-ethnic conflict in the territory of the Russian Federation, in which refugees actively participated. In the political aspect, refugees are an extremely unstable part of the population, with changeable political views and orientations. They have nothing to lose, and thus it is very likely that they may support reactionary forces that promise them 'the good life in a land of plenty'.

Refugees and forced migrants, as well as other groups of migrants (people that were moved from the Chernobyl region after the nuclear disaster, retired military servicemen, former residents of the northern territories, rehabilitated nations) almost always prompt a negative reaction among the local population, which blames them for low living standards, price increases and other hardships. This is so because newcomers need accommodation, employment and social protection, all of which is insufficient for the local population as it is. Thus, the probability of inter-ethnic conflicts and the growth of criminality becomes higher with the inflow of migrants, especially if they do not belong to the native nationality. Certainly, in most cases this is just a groundless search for scapegoats and none of these events are directly connected with forced migrants. According to the reports of the Ministry of Internal Affairs, crime rates among refugees do not exceed the average level.

Yet at the same time, the situation in the North Caucasus is becoming even tenser and this is directly connected with the refugees from the 'Caucasian nations' – Azerbaidzhani, Ossetians, Assyrians and especially Armenians.

The acuteness of problems caused by the inflow of refugees depends on their share in the population of the region. According to the adopted standards, an extreme level of tension has been registered only in North Ossetia as a result of the inflow of refugees (they make up 17% of the population). Among other regions, Stavropol' and Krasnodar *krais* and Belgorod, Voronezh, Saratov, Orenburg and Kaluga *oblasts* experience the most serious impact of the refugee problem. In these regions the share of refugees and migrants exceeds 1%. Tension caused by them is very high, as is the probability of social and inter-ethnic conflict.

However, in comparison with other countries of the world, the number of migrants and their share in the total number of the Russian population is not very high. Undoubtedly, the situation in some independent states – the FSU republics – is much more difficult.

These republics, in the same way as Russia, suffered from the national policy that had been implemented for years, but now they are in a more difficult situation because of economic hardships and armed clashes on their territory. However, the number of refugees and migrants in these independent states may be compared to that in Russia, though these countries have a much smaller area and population. Thus, according to official data there are over 1 million forced migrants in Azerbaidzhan, 502,000 in Armenia (14% of the population), over 350,000 in Tadzhikistan and over 200,000 in Georgia[5]. Taken alone, these figures show that the problems, which these FSU states are facing seem to be more complicated than those of Russia.

Another important difference is that in Russia, most migrants do not face problems of language and cultural adaptation because all of them are Russian-speakers and have for a long time lived in a common informational and cultural environment, whereas this is a real problem for most of the independent states.

Refugees and migrants that have arrived in Russia were mostly residents of big cities and had worked in the fields of industry, science, education and medicine.

---

5 Rybakovskii, L.L., and N.V. Tarasova. „Vnutrirossiiskaya migratsiya naseleniya: nyneshnyaya situatsiya i prognoz [Migration of Population inside Russia: Present Situation and Forecasts]." *Sotsis* 1994, no. 1.

Their level of education is high (almost every seventh has higher education) and they have good professional skills. If properly used, their potential might be very useful for Russia. However, as analysis of the activity of the state migration service and study of migration programmes reveal, it is too early to speak of the effective use of the newcomers' working potential.

6 State Policy of Settling Refugees and Migrants

State policy for protection of refugees and migrants includes several aspects. Among them there is the drafting of new laws and programmes, determination of places of temporary and permanent residence, transportation, settlement, employment, financial and informational support. None of these problems have been resolved as yet, because the laws, though they have been passed, are of a mainly declarative nature. The mechanism of their implementation has not been worked out, transportation aid is granted only in extreme cases, financial support and assistance in solving immediate problems of settlement are inadequate: only refugees and migrants that live below the poverty limit (single pensioners, disabled persons, families with many children) are granted one minimal salary as aid (two minimal salaries in rural areas); migrants are also granted the right to receive a long-term (10 years) interest-free repayable loan for buying (or building) a house which amounts to 700,000 roubles per person (from October 1993). Naturally, this is not sufficient. Thus, the FMS has calculated that if the provisions of the law *On Refugees* were observed, 43 million roubles (at the prices of January 1994) would be required for each individual. Providing effective aid to refugees becomes difficult because of economic hardships, inadequate funding and insufficient staff, especially in the provinces. In 1993 alone, over 150,000 migrants below the poverty limit received grants (1-2 minimal salaries), 9,700 families received loans for the construction of homes, 92 villages are under construction, 24 centres of temporary accommodation for 4,500 people have been set up in peaceful areas, as well as shelters for 14,000 people in areas of inter-ethnic conflicts.

State policy on how to treat forced migrants is only just being formed. The main provisions of this policy are laid out in the federal migration programme which was drafted by the FMS and approved by presidential decree on 9 August 1994. The programme proclaims worthwhile and humane tasks but, unfortunately, it also contains some conceptual mistakes which may cause suffering for many years ahead. This applies first of all to the underlying principle of the migration policy – the organised attraction of population for the revival of thinly populated regions and villages (especially in non-black-earth areas). In places where expansion of industry and agriculture is impossible, settling migrants is considered inexpedient.

It is difficult to agree with this approach since it looks as an attempt to solve state problems at the expense of refugees and migrants – such problems as developing new lands, re-colonisation of certain territories, as though the negative and expensive experience of the 'revival of the non-black-earth lands' has been forgotten. If someone seriously wanted to solve the problem of such important regions as the North and 'non-black earth' land, then it would be more efficient to direct funds towards their stabilisation and stem the flow of migrants from these areas. It is more reasonable to restore to the native population the privileges that were cancelled than to introduce new ones for the refugees.

It is worth considering once again whether it is reasonable to develop new lands and expand production areas, particularly in central Russia. Perhaps it would be better to use the skills and energy of the migrants for the reconstruction and modernisation of enterprises, for constructing new 'public' car plants, roadways or, for instance, a high-speed railway from Moscow to St. Petersburg. It might be wise to use migrants for the development of services in cities, including resorts and historical towns, many of which die out without fresh inflow of population.

Undoubtedly, there is a considerable deficit of manpower in villages and it is quite obvious that it is impossible to develop rural areas without attracting additional labour resources. It is certainly easier to 'survive' in villages, as it is easier to find accommodation there and subsist on self-catering. However, this all needs funding, and it would be naive to count on the migrants to build up their own profitable farms because this activity requires huge funds, connections, skills and help, which are not available even to the native people living in the countryside. One should not forget that in all ethnic republics, Russians used to live mainly in capital cities and were members of elites, therefore their re-orientation to agriculture is rather problematic.

While migrants are being persistently offered places in 'the heart of the country', many workers from other states are attracted to Russian cities. According to official data only, there are 330-400,000 foreign workers in Russia having mainly arrived from the FSU republics of Ukraine, Belarus and Moldova. The FMS recently issued hundreds of permits to attract 80,000 workers. All of them go to cities were they find accommodation, however lack of accommodation for refugees and migrants is a constant problem.

Another disputable question is that of the planned quotas and restrictions in choosing places of residence for the refugees (but not for migrants). This is a rather common practice in the world, however the application of such rules is contrary both to the Russian Constitution and Russian laws. Furthermore, restricting the right of refugees to reside in certain areas requires that the State fulfils many of its obligations, creates new structures, considerably enlarges the staff of the migration service, i.e., such restrictions require substantial funding.

The above-mentioned makes measures outlined by the programme very disputable, although it is too early to make any final judgements. Many of the provisions of the programme have started to be implemented at the local level in Pskov, Novgorod, Orel and Tambov *oblasts* with due regard to specific local conditions.

These regional programmes are very progressive and encouraging because they show deviation from the principle of a common policy, controlled by the Centre, towards a more decentralised regional policy. Pskov *oblast'* should be mentioned separately, since the *oblast'* administration suggested that it be assigned the status of a 'base territory' for receiving refugees from the CIS states, Baltic republics and the Far North. The regional resettlement programme stipulates for 1994-98 a complex set of measures aimed at settling and providing favourable living conditions for 10,000 people. Three variants are suggested: individual settling and employment; compact settling and employment; compact settling and creation of production and business associations of resettlers. The resettlers shall be free to make their choice according to their skills, preferences and funds available[6].

It is always desirable (and especially if the funds are limited) to be oriented towards minimal expenditure. When settling forced migrants, the principle of 'if you can't help, then at least don't get in the way' must be observed. The desire of refugees and migrants to quickly adjust themselves to the new environment should be considered; they ought to be given greater freedom to choose their place of residence and employment; people from cities (who are mostly skilled specialists) should not be forcibly sent to boost Russian agriculture.

State policy towards refugees and migrants is not limited to the activities of the FMS, but includes many aspects of activity of other state bodies and public institutions. Sadly, numerous public organisations have limited possibilities and their

---

6 Filippova, E. „Varianty naydeny, voprosy ostayutsya. Rasmyshleniya po povodu pskovskoy programmy 'Pereseleniye' [Variants Found -- Questions Remain: Some Thoughts about the Pskov 'Resettling' Programme]." *Vash Vybor* 1993, no. 6.

actions are not well co-ordinated. Neither are they in agreement with the FMS, with whom many public organisations are in conflict. The participation of the Russian Orthodox Church in receiving and taking care of forced migrants is inadequate.

Activity aimed at organising links between the FSU republics in their attempts to solve the problem of refugees and migrants, as well as with regard to protection of rights of Russians living outside Russia is a special issue of the migration policy. There is a need for such activity but, unfortunately, agreements signed concerning these problems between states are relatively ineffective. Furthermore, discrimination against Russian-speakers at official levels is not particularly far-reaching (except, perhaps, in Latvia and Estonia). The forcing out of Russians takes place at the level of everyday life which cannot be regulated either by agreements, or by political claims. However successful the policy of support of ethnic Russians in the CIS countries may be, the process of their return continues and cannot be stopped.

In any event, Russia must be prepared to accept any citizen of the former Soviet Union refraining from turning migrants into refugees, and provide them with decent living conditions in their new environment.

4

Social Stratification of Belarussian Society: Situation and Tendencies of Development

Anatolii Makarov

1 Fundamental Principles and Criteria for the Analysis of Social Stratification in Belarussian Society

The term 'social stratification' can be translated into Russian as 'social structure'. The concept of social stratification has been widely used by several generations of scientists the whole world over.

Unfortunately, the above-mentioned theory and methods of measuring social stratification had been practically neglected in the former USSR. However, this does not of course mean that the priorities of today's agenda do not include the analysis and comparison of the social structure of the post-Soviet states, as well as the identification of specific features in their modernisation process and the assessment of the possibilities of their social integration into the world community. In this context it is expedient to define the fundamental principles and the criteria for analysing the social structure of Belarussian society.

2 General Indicators

In the West, the generally accepted definition of social stratification is the fixation of the structural inequality between different groups of people.

The modern approach to social stratification has as its foundation theoretical research by Max Weber. Weber identifies three factors upon which the system of stratification is built:

- division of society into classes (according to the property, qualification and skills of an individual);
- status of an individual (or a group);
- relation of an individual to power (party membership).

These factors are regarded as the general indicators of social differentiation. Today the best known and most developed is the functional conception of social stratification (Parsons, Sheels, B.Barber, C.Davis, Y.Moore). Its fundamental principles are: that the system of social stratification is the result of differentiation of roles and positions within the given society. That differentiation is determined on the one hand by the division of labour and social distinction of various groups and on the other hand it is the result of the predominant system of values and standards, which legitimises the existing social inequality. The functional approach postulates that social stratification promotes societal integration when accompanied by a rational system of incentives. Parson's theory of social action identifies three universal criteria for social stratification:

- quality (responsibility, competence);
- performance (comparative assessment of the results of individuals' activities);
- 'possession' of material values, talent, advanced skills and cultural resources.

Finally, on the level of empirical sociology, when applying the so-called 'objective approach' to the analyses of social stratification one usually focuses on class structure of society and uses the concept of socio-economic status, which normally includes three variables:

- prestige of profession;
- educational level;
- income level.

To what extent could the above-mentioned principles, approaches and criteria be applied to the analyses of social stratification of Belarussian society? Broadly speaking it is possible to say that correct application of those theoretical tools depends on the degree of their correlation with the real structure of Belarussian society, with the real values, norms and traditions regarding social inequality.

2.1 Relative 'Structurelessness' of Belarussian Society

According to the theory of social stratification, modern western society can be divided into four classes: the upper class, the middle class, the working class and the peasants. In turn, the middle class is traditionally subdivided into the upper and the lower layers, as is the working class. This structure of western society is determined by the fact that socio-economic resources are not shared on an equal basis by these large groups of people, which significantly influences their living standards and their lifestyles.

Supposing that a similar division of Belarussian society is possible, we cannot, however, draw straight parallels between the two societies. Why is this so? Firstly, because the social structures of the former republics of the USSR had been formed under conditions and in traditions totally different from western standards. In particular, the prevailing form of property had been 'public' property in its two variants: state-owned property and that owned by co-operatives. Accordingly, the greater part of the population was in fact employed by the state which owned all main resources and assets. The present situation in post-Soviet Belarussian society is not greatly different, although some changes have actually taken place.

These changes primarily concern the increase during the *perestroika*-period in the proportion of the population that works for enterprises and organisations under collective ownership.

Table 1 *Proportion of working population by form of ownership (in %)*

	1985	1993
State entreprises and organisations	81	63
Individual and private entrepreneurship	1	5
Entreprises and organisations with collective ownership	18	30
Organisations and entreprises with mixed forms of ownership (including foreign)	0	2

It should be mentioned that a considerable part of the population employed in enterprises under collective ownership works in such traditional forms as kolkhozes (agricultural co-operatives) and co-operatives. Other forms of collective ownership (joint-stock companies, lease) are as yet in the initial stages of development.

Private property is also at an early stage of formation. In general it can be ascertained that the prevailing part of the urban workforce is employed in the state sector or in the sectors dependent on it, and the countryside inhabitants are employed mostly in kolkhozes and sovkhozes (state-owned agricultural co-operatives). Therefore it is premature to talk about stratification of the Belarussian population according to forms of ownership.

As far as social status is concerned, the prestige of occupations and professions varied over decades with predominant official ideologies. Thus the social status of the working class as a social leader and as the 'most advanced' class was turned into a stereotype actively Forced upon the mentality of society. As for the intelligentsia, it was merely given the minor role of a social layer, which did not reflect the real role it played in society. At the same time the ruling elite always enjoyed an elevated social status regardless of the ideological slogans.

If we consider such a universal indicator of social stratification as income level we can observe that in the post-*perestroika* period almost every stratum of the Belarussian population suffered from a shocking instability. Income rates have not only plummeted, but have become virtually impossible to predict for some social groups and layers.

Thus, compared to the modern western societies Belarussian society is characterised by a different initial state, different traditions and peculiarities of social stratification.

2.2 Transitional Condition of Society

Just like other CIS countries, Belarus is in a transitional state. What is characteristic of the transitional processes in Belarus? The moods and expectations of the Belarussian population are strongly dominated by stereotypes of social security, often misunderstood as socialist egalitarianism. In this connection, hopes that the state will protect the people against bankruptcies of enterprises and mass unemployment even in the case of severe economic crisis are strong.

Simultaneously, there are signs of new tendencies in the development of Belarus: mixed economy, market relations, private property and so forth. Socialist orientations coexist with other values even in the programmes of political parties. Similar to that is the behaviour of some politicians. Concrete guidelines for social development as well as a model of socio-economic policy are not yet worked out at the legislative level. The instability that characterises transformation processes in the Republic of Belarus makes it difficult to analyse social stratification, especially with respect to the identification of current tendencies. However, some indicators of the real situation among classes, social and professional groups and strata can be clarified.

3 Major Classes and Strata of Belarussian Society

Taking into account the above-mentioned principles and peculiarities of the analysis of social stratification it is possible to give the characteristics of every major class and stratum of Belarussian society. We proceed from the assumption that classes and strata of Belarussian society can not be fixed within a stable framework of a number of indicators (property – income level; status – prestige; relation to power;

educational level; qualifications – creative potential; complexity of work and other). Analysing some strata it is possible to identify clusters of indicators peculiar to that given stratum alone. Other strata can be identified by means of one or two indicators, which give us sufficient grounds for that identification at the present stage of transformation of the social structure of Belarus.

3.1 The Elite

At the present, transformational stage of development, elite groups have acquired special importance in Belarus, as their position and actions determine how fast and in what direction the post-totalitarian modernisation will go.

The Belarussian elite phenomenon in the context of the social structure of society has some specific features.

Firstly, elite groups retained their dominance over the socio-economic life of the country during the whole stretch of the post-*perestroika* period. Some of them have continuously been trying to monopolise political power. Prior to the recent presidential elections, the political monopoly belonged to the so-called 'party of power' which served the interests of the prime minister, V.Kebitch and his team, and reflected their position. After the presidential elections these are A.Lukashenko and his team, who represent the executive branch of power, trying to steer the post-totalitarian development of Belarus.

Secondly, presidential power is a new phenomenon for Belarus. Presidential power was born in the course of political fighting between the 'old' and the 'new *nomenklatura*' A.Lukashenko's victory at the elections has brought a new political elite into top echelons of executive power, younger in age (40-50 years old). Lukashenko's team are as a rule people of technical education who worked in Parliament or in the Council of Ministers.

Having formed the top elite layer, presidential power has recently acquired the possibility of recruiting elites at the level of local authorities. The creation of the president's vertical chain of power is now complete: the chairmen of the executive committees of the regional, district and city soviets are all appointed. Thus, local executive authorities are all directly subordinate to the president. The presidential power structure is becoming multi-layered, embracing governing elites at all levels. The mode of action of these elites will have a significant influence on socio-political processes in Belarus, determining their direction.

Thirdly, another feature of elite stratification of Belarussian society is the process of dividing power into the legislative, executive and judicial branches, which has now commenced. As a result, rivalry between different political elites sparks up. This rivalry is particularly pronounced at the level of political competition between presidential (executive) and legislative powers (Parliament). This competition, if the democratic rules of the political game are not violated, could avert the danger of monopolisation of power in the future.

The supreme judicial power of Belarus as an independent political force came into being in 1994. The Constitutional Court carried out an analysis of the state of enforcement of constitutional laws and pronounced its judgements addressing legislative and executive organs.

Among the issues covered by the analysis are issues of the legal defence of citizens in the sphere of labour, civil and administrative problems, the degree of conformity of some of the norms of criminal law with the constitution, equal legal guarantees for all forms of ownership, conformity with the constitution of the amendments concerning local self-government and other issues. The Constitutional Court has also put forward some proposals for the revision of the existing procedures of law-making. The first steps made by the Constitutional Court will surely shake up the judicial branch at all levels. This is a prerequisite for the appearance of a relatively independent political elite which could administer arbitration and protect the law in the corridors of power.

Fourthly, elite roles also belong to those groups in Belarussian society which possess some form of significant resources. These are the top managers of the Belarussian industrial and agricultural sectors, influential financial and commercial structures. These elite groups have, as a rule, their lobby within the government and the presidential elections were much influenced by them. These groups will seek to get their candidates into the *Supreme Soviet* during the coming parliamentary elections in order to ensure the presence of their own, legalised lobby.

Fifthly, into a separate category fall the elites which have spiritual and ideological resources. These are the elite strata represented by political parties and movements. In that context we can also talk about 'anti-elites'. These are the political parties which contest political power and promote alternative programmes of socio-economic reforms. They include the democratic bloc (the Belarussian *National Front*, the Belarussian *Social Democrats*, the Belarussian *Christian Democratic Party*, the Belarussian *Peasant Party*, the *National-Democratic Party of Belarus*); the *Civil Accord* bloc (the *Party of National Accord*, the *United Democratic Party of Belarus*, the *Civil Party*, the *Geopolitics, Integration and Progress* Association.

The above-mentioned specific features of stratification of Belarussian society lead us to the conclusion that the social status and position of different elite groups within the establishment are not stable. The next one to two years will witness shifts and recombinations of these elite groups. That will primarily be connected with the struggle for power both at top and local levels.

3.2 The Working Class

General characteristics: The estimated number of workers in Belarus in 1993 was 2,522,000 or 57.1% of the active working population of the republic. The majority of them are industrial workers, their number reaching 1,138,000 in 1994.

Social status: In the post-*perestroika* period the stereotype of working class hegemony has fallen dramatically. However, the actual role and social status of the working class in Belarus are still significant. This is so for several reasons. Firstly, it is the largest social group in the structure of the active population, with workers constituting two-thirds of all employees in the state sector of the economy. Secondly, their contribution in the gross national product is still the biggest. The output of intellectual products and the service sector can not yet compete in any way with traditional material production, that provides the majority of workers in Belarus with employment. Thirdly, the working class is the best organised social group in the republic in terms of protecting their economic interests and political actions. This has become clear after the recent strikes, meetings and in the wake of the organisation of an independent trade-union. The traditionally high status of the working class is likely to be preserved in the near future as the pace of restructuring of economy is sluggish.

Income level: There are no differentiated statistics on the income level of workers, yet taking into account that the majority of them are employed in production, we can make some comparisons. Thus, in 1993 the monthly salary of workers and employees in industry amounted to 61,389 roubles, whereas the salary of those working in the sphere of education was no more than 46,911 roubles.

Just as within other categories, among workers there are some groups with low income. It must be taken into account that income depends now on the profitability of an enterprise. About one-third of all enterprises are loss-makers. Holiday without pay and shortened working weeks are widely used measures. Despite the fact that the state subsidises loss-making enterprises, the threat of mass unemployment is becoming more and more real. For this reason the relatively high salaries of a section of workers no longer reflect the well-being of the working class as a whole.

Relation to power: In the post-*perestroika* years the working class of Belarus manifested itself as a force to be reckoned with in governmental circles. All kinds of politicians and political parties appeal and try to make advances to that force.

Many workers stand firmly for anti-corruption measures and oppose the 'old *nomenklatura*'. The Belarussian *National Front*, an opposition party, is also largely supported by the working class. In addition, Belarussian workers are inclined to give their support to those political figures and parties that promise them state provided social security.

As far as political involvement is concerned, the working class is not homogeneous. The most active participants in political processes are the workers of large industrial enterprises, transport workers, machine builders and miners.

The outcome of the future parliamentary elections will very much depend on the position taken by the majority of workers.

3.3 The Farmers

General characteristics: Since 1970 annual population growth in Belarus has risen to 4% and, at the same time, the size of the rural population dropped by 13%. The number of those working in kolkhozes and sovkhozes decreased by 45%. The majority of peasants work in these enterprises. In 1993 kolkhozes embraced 551,500 people and sovkhozes – 188,000 people.

At the same time, first steps are being made by Belarussian farmers. The dynamics of their growth and major performance indicators are given in table 1.

Table 2 *Farm holdings (including private farms) on 1 January 1994*

	1992	1993	1994
Number of farm holdings	757	2372	27303
Area available for agricultural plots ('000 ha)	15.6	45.6	55.8
including for grazing:	10.3	29.1	36.1
Average size of agricultural plots arable land (ha)	20.6	19.2	20.4
grazing land (ha)	13.6	12.3	13.4

Farmers in Belarus now face unfavourable conditions, their production potential is low and, as a result, they have only a slight impact on the reform process affecting the traditional collective forms of ownership in the countryside. The following data prove this:

The area of land belonging to farmers at the beginning of 1994 was only 0.6% of the total agricultural lands in the republic. On average, every 10 farmers have 20 head of cattle (11 of which are cows), 25 pigs, 2 horses, 11 tractors and 3 trucks. Only one in every 7 farms has a grain harvester, one-quarter of farms have sowing-machines, one-third of farms have potato-planters and potato-diggers.

It is obvious that the future of farmers will depend on a state policy that would address their needs.

Social status: Peasants' work has always been lacking in terms of prestige, both in the Soviet and in the post-Soviet Belarus. The reasons for that are the poor working conditions and low consumption of material and spiritual goods as compared with the urban population. Today this situation of village-city inequality is not much different (discrepancy in prices for industrial and agricultural products, residual supply of material and energy resources, subsidies and consumer goods to rural areas after the needs of cities are satisfied).

It much also be taken into account that collectivisation under Stalin had badly ravaged the ranks of the hard-working and the well-to-do in peasant class, with the post-war rural exodus aggravating that situation.

The social status of peasants has gradually risen in recent years against the background of general deterioration of the economic situation in Belarus. The fact that every rural household has at its disposal a small plot of land and that that land yields more than the household consumes makes their work more significant and rewarding and also helps them to survive the difficulties of the current economic crisis. better than the city population. At the same time there is a gradually growth of city-to-village migration as the threat of mass unemployment and the ever-growing cost of living in the cities force such a return.

Income level: The average monthly salary of kolkhoz workers in 1993 was 42,587 roubles, that of sovkhoz workers was 46,847 roubles. In comparison, the average monthly salary of industrial workers in 1993 was 62,215 roubles.

Incomes of the rural population are not limited to the money that they receive from the state or from a co-operative as their salary. Peasants also profit from the selling of their agricultural products privately using their small plots of land and the farming facilities that every rural household normally possesses.

Research into the family budgets of peasants gives the following structure of their income.

Table 3 *Composition of combined family income of kolhoz-farmers and its use (in %)*

	1990	1991	1992	1993
Combined income - total	100	100	100	100
Composition of income:				
• income from the kolkhoz	54.1	43.1	34.0	33.1
• wage of family members	6.0	5.6	4.8	4.8
• pensions, stipends, various allowances	13.3	21.0	15.6	12.2
• income from personal subsidiary farm holding	23.6	27.1	42.6	46.3
• income from other sources	3.0	3.0	3.0	3.6
Outlays:				
• Food	30.4	32.1	47.0	49.3
• Non-food goods	24.3	27.1	23.2	20.1
• Family savings	20.1	20.0	13.0	13.5

The average sum of deposits in savings banks can serve as an indirect indicator of the income level of peasants in comparison to other social groups. On average, the deposit in saving banks per capita in cities and towns was 27,460 roubles and in rural areas it was only 18,849 roubles.

Relation to power: In political terms, Belarussian peasants are the most indifferent social group. This can be explained by the conditions and the mode of their life, by the structure of their time budget and by their educational and cultural levels. Being much more dependent on the local authorities (kolkhoz managers, foremen etc.) than the urban population, they traditionally support the political line indicated to them and approved by their local authorities.

In the course of Belorussia's first presidential election campaign the peasants showed for the first time certain political activity as well as a range of political orientations and preferences of their own. It is interesting that despite the propaganda and pressure from the 'party of power' (the cabinet), many rural electors voted not for V.Kebitch but for A.Lukashenko. The same differentiated political behaviour is likely to be seen during the forthcoming parliamentary elections. The peasants have started to wake up.

3.4 White Collar Workers

General characteristics: According to western classification, white collar workers – intellectuals of all professions and qualifications – belong in their majority to the middle class. There is no distinct middle class in Belarus as yet. As for the people whose activity is connected with intellectual labour, their composition is not homogenous, and they fall into two main categories: the intelligentsia and office workers.

Soviet ideology attributed to the intelligentsia all those who carry out professionally highly qualified intellectual work requiring higher or specialised secondary education.

For their part, the office workers are those who carry out low or medium qualification intellectual work not requiring higher or specialised secondary education. Office workers as a sociological layer must not be confused with public employees as a statistical category, for example those who carry out intellectual work and who are employed by the state.

1994 statistics registered 1,348,800 white collar workers ('brain workers') in the economy of Belarus or 30% of the total work force. 302,100 of them are managers of all levels and 913,000 are technical specialists. Therefore, taken together these two groups of white collar workers constitute a large part of the active work force of the republic.

Social status: Along with the official stereotype regarding white collar workers as a minor social layer, there had always been another stereotype, coexistent with the first one: the intelligentsia are highly educated people and it is extremely desirable that our children join them. Despite a comparatively low income at the first stages of their career, the intelligentsia could always count on the eventual improvement of their material situation and a prestigious position in society as they gained experience and climbed up the ladder.

The social status of the intelligentsia sharply declined over the *perestroika* years. Commercialisation of social life of the population of Belarus made it fashionable to make 'easy money' through buying and reselling, on shuttle trips abroad and so forth. This resulted in a new stereotype image that one can get rich very quickly and live a life of luxury without spending many years on education.

The state has not managed to provide any social security for the intelligentsia, to protect that group from the adversities of economic crisis and to maintain the balance of their income with that of other social groups.

Income level: White collar workers employed in non-production branches of the economy have found themselves in the most difficult situation. While the average monthly salary of those working in industry in 1993 was 62,215 roubles, the average salary of medical personnel, PE teachers and social security employees was 47,060 roubles, teachers received a monthly 46,911 roubles, employees in cultural sphere –

41,309 roubles, those working in the sphere of state-subsidised art 40,551 roubles and scientific research workers – 55,626 roubles.

Relation to power: The political activity of the Belarussian intelligentsia increased considerably in the *perestroika* and post-*perestroika* years. White collar workers are now characterised by active participation in discussions, meetings, strikes and the organisation of election campaigns.

Many people belonging to the intelligentsia have integrated into the political process and are now trying to redistribute power or to influence power structures. Dozens of newly created parties and political movements are the reflection of that process. Such parties and movements as the Belarussian *National Front*, the Belarussian *Social-Democratic Party*, the *Party of National Accord* and some others have their own alternative national development programmes, shadow cabinets or analogous structures.

A new generation of managers and politicians is reinforcing the new national power structure. It is characteristic of the present period that such categories of the intelligentsia as economists, sociologists, politologists and lawyers are being recruited by power structures (the presidential administration, the Council of Ministers, the Supreme Soviet, organs of local authorities). Intellectuals and professionals now have a real opportunity to influence political processes in the republic.

Simultaneously, the decline of incomes and social status affecting many other categories of white collar workers makes them radicalise their political actions. This can be illustrated by the stance adopted by the national education workers who participated actively in the pickets and meetings during sessions of the Supreme Soviet, also announcing their intention to go on strike themselves.

It is evident that the position and actions of the intelligentsia will continue to influence the political process in Belarus.

3.5 The Middle Class: Sources and Stages of Formation

During the Soviet period a certain section of the highly qualified strata of the working class could have been regarded as the middle class. The social status and income level of these groups suggest that the name 'middle class' could with a slight reservation be applied to these strata.

The post-*perestroika* transformations and instability have made border lines within the social structure of society less distinct and now we can talk about the formation of the middle class only as a possibility in the future.

According to some estimates, about 15% of the population of the former republics of the USSR can potentially start the formation of the middle class. What are the supposed sources of its formation?

In the first instance, these are those people who are now in possession of certain property. These are the businessmen and the farmers. The middle class can also grow at the expense of a large number of specialists who have higher and specialised secondary education. This will happen, of course, only if their incomes would correspond to the complexity and significance of the work they do.

Other sources that can contribute to the middle class are the civil servants who form the bureaucratic machinery of the state, top managers, commercial workers and others.

At the same time, specific socio-economic relations in Belarus demand that the middle class of the republic reaches maturity step by step. In conjunction with the gradual creation of a legislative base regulating free enterprise, the parallel transformation of Belarussian enterprises into joint-stock companies is becoming a possibility. While the principle of wage-levelling, egalitarianism and even the deliberate underrating of the social status of some categories of employees remains in common use up to this date, the issue of legitimising the system of differentiated payment according to the degree of complexity and significance of work will inevitably be put on the agenda.

On the whole, successful formation of the middle class will depend on the political line chosen by the government.

3.6 Marginal Elements and Marginalism in Society

Marginalism in the theory of social stratification means that some people in society do not belong to any of the social groups and find themselves on the edge of strata, or, as it were, in the in-between position.

The classical example of this is a rural dweller who has migrated into a city. All his economic, social and psychological ties with his social community are disrupted. The loss of self-identification with a certain social group, erosion of moral standards and values inherited by the migrant from the subculture that he originated from and his failure to eventually integrate into a new subculture – these are the main features that constitute the essence of marginalization.

Members of any society can find themselves in a marginal state through conscious choice or as a result of unfavourable circumstances, either forced by economic crisis or the social policies of the state. As the French researcher A.Farge points out, it is characteristic of modern society that the marginality of those alienated from their native surroundings is a product of a society afflicted by crisis[1].

The phenomenon of marginalism applied to the social structure of society signifies the erosion of its class fabric, social instability and the appearance of potential hotbeds of tension and conflicts.

The problem of social marginalism in Belarus is becoming more and more serious under the pressure of the present socio-economic and political crisis. Who exactly are the marginal elements in Belarus?

The *registered unemployed* form the most evident category of marginal elements to be studied. The dynamics of unemployment growth are given in table 3.

The unemployment rate in Belarus for the first half of 1994 was 1.58%. 63% of the unemployed belong to the working class and 37% are office workers.

Table 4 *Number of unemployed in Belarus (people)*

	Registered unemployed (total)	Number of unemployed receiving assistance
1 January 1991	331	171
1 January 1992	3368	1557
1 July 1992	7056	5329
1 January 1993	24014	19940
1 July 1993	54832	27399
1 January 1994	66329	34513
January 1 1995	102391	

These numbers are, however, only the tip of the iceberg. Today, one-third of Belorussia's active population is affected by hidden unemployment. Thus, we have a precedent of latent mass marginality. Hundreds of thousands of people have their usual consumption level sharply cut and their social status is becoming unstable. This results in their readiness for radical actions to support those politicians and political forces who make them any promises. The recent presidential elections can serve as a graphic illustration of that.

Special attention must be given to that section of the Belarussian population who traditionally held the elite position in society, both from the point of view of their incomes and social status. In particular, this concerns *officers in the armed forces*, with the social status of a significant of them becoming very uncertain and unpredictable. The reduction of the military forces in Belarus pushed many categories of military specialists onto the labour market. It must also be taken into

1 Arlet Farzh. „Marginaly [Marginals]." In *50/50. Opyt slovarya novogo myshleniya* [Essay on the Vocabulary of the New Thinking]. Moscow, 1989.

account that tens of thousands of families of military officers have no apartments. This all combines to create an atmosphere of social uncertainly, marginality and dissatisfaction with the official social policy.

Marginal conditions and marginal attitudes are noticeable among *teachers* (especially those teaching humanitarian subjects) and *scientific research workers*. As a result, many research workers abandoned the scientific field for others such as business and commerce. Another consequence of this situation is the radicalisation of social and political attitudes of the intelligentsia.

The problem of marginalism is aggravated by *immigrants* from neighbouring countries. 47.2% of the immigrants who arrived in Belarus from the countries of the former USSR in 1993 are Belarussians, 36.1% are Russians, 9% are Ukrainians, 2.1% are Poles, 0.4% are Jews and 5.1% are people of other nationalities. These figures show that the majority of the immigrants are nationally and ethnically close to the population of Belarus, a fact which considerably facilitates their adaptation to their new place of residence. So far, no alarming incidents related to immigration in Belarus have been recorded.

Finally, the specific *'non-classical' marginalism* must be pointed out. This is manifested in the shift or complete loss of traditional socio-psychological patterns of behaviour and ideological orientations in the public consciousness. The reasons for this are evident: political power in the republic is not stable enough to efficiently steer the reform process. The absence of guaranteed social security, the threat of mass unemployment, the search for new ideological formulas and the not-yet-completed adaptation to pluralism and democracy are also adding fuel to the fire. As a result, the old codes of honesty and conscientiousness of work are being neglected in many social groups. Norms of professionalism are also deteriorating. A double standard effect is observed when a person who formally belongs to a certain professional group or collective does not consider the traditional values and norms of behaviour accepted there as binding for him.

The above-mentioned problems and tendencies connected with marginalism in Belarussian society jeopardise its social and political stability and carry a potential threat to the process of democratisation and transformation taking place in Belarus.

4 The Rich and the Poor: The Problem of Social Polarisation

Indicators of social stratification conventional in the countries of the West can not be fully applied to Belarussian society for one more reason beyond those mentioned above: the levelling of incomes of the greater part of the active population. It would be even more correct to say that many strata which differ in terms of their social status are approaching the poverty line and even cross it as their incomes continue to fall. At present over five million people (more than 50%) in Belarus live below the poverty line.

Such indicator as 'income level' is apparently becoming indicator number one for assessing social stratification of Belarussian society. It seems that in the nearest future it will be more expedient to compare the strata using the following two indicators: the percentage of the population with incomes at the level of the minimal serviceable consumption (MSC) and the percentage of those who live below the poverty line (with the poverty line fixed at 60% of the MSC).

As a result of mass impoverishment, public opinion places in the category of 'the rich' both those who have really high incomes (legal or illegal) and those whose incomes barely exceed the level of the MSC. This creates the basis for a social outbreak that might be directed both against the government and 'the rich'.

This is just another proof of both the danger of underestimating the 'buffer' role of the middle class in a socially cleaved society and of the urgency of prompt economic reforms.

The negative consequences of the social polarisation of Belarussian society are being mitigated to a certain extent by the people themselves. In particular, if in 1990 only 14.9% of the aggregate family income came from private activities, in 1993 this share reached 27.4%. It must also be taken into account that many city inhabitants have relatives in the country and that the people living in small towns and villages usually have small plots of land that they cultivate and certain farming facilities that they use. Similarly, a large number of urban dwellers have dachas – small country houses on a small plot of land. In other words, a sharp fall in income forces a significant part of the population to provide themselves with agricultural products through their own efforts and means. On the whole, this merely relieves the problem of mass impoverishment rather than solving it, and it also does not diminish ever-growing social dissatisfaction.

5 Tendencies in Social Stratification of Belarussian Society: Probability of the Possible

Analysis and observation of the course that the social stratification in Belarus is taking provide the grounds for making some generalisations and conclusions about the tendencies of that process.

5.1 'Structurelessness' of society

The relative structurelessness of Belarussian society is likely to remain for several years to come as the radical restructuring of the economy is not yet in sight. Even with the reforms already underway, it will take some time for strata identical with the western ones to take shape.

5.2 Conservatism of strata

Conservative stereotypes held by the majority of those employed in the state or the kolkhoz sectors with regard to forms of ownership can be expected to remain.

The working class and the peasants embraced by kolkhozes (i.e. collective farms) will support the policy directed at preserving these sectors as the predominant sectors of the economy.

Pensioners, women and other categories of the population can also be expected to take a conservative position with regard to the social policy of the state, that is they are likely to support the socialist, egalitarian type of social security system.

5.3 Fluctuations of strata

Using the terminology of Peterim Sorokin, who is one of the founders of modern American sociology, it is possible to prognosticate the probability of fluctuations in the socio-economic status of different classes and strata[2]. The first type of fluctuations is related to an economic fall or rise of a social group. As for the upcoming stage of development of Belarussian society, it can be presumed that the fall of the socio-economic status and the income level of the major classes and strata will continue as a tendency. Government programmes, including those on unemployment, can only partially compensate for that fall. Another compensation

---

2 Sorokin, P. "Sotsial'naya stratifikatsiya i mobil'nost' [Social Stratification and Mobility]." In *Chelovek. Tsivilizatsiya. Obshchestvo* [Man. Civilisation. Society]. Moscow, 1992.

factor is represented by the attempts that are being made by the majority of the population to find an additional income beyond that brought in by the principal job. An economical lifestyle and self-provision with agricultural products also serve as a certain compensation. Political fluctuations under these circumstances can become aimless and can cause frequent changes of public opinion in favour of this or that political figure or force.

The second type of fluctuations makes it possible to draw a socio-economic profile within a concrete group. Prognostication of the profile and the trend of the major strata of Belarussian society is difficult because of several reasons. Firstly, whereas certain classes and strata taken as a whole can be identified and a fall in their well-being can be predicted, within these classes there is a highly mobile economic differentiation. For instance, within the working class in Belarus there are considerable differences in incomes even between similar socio-professional groups working at different enterprises. This difference in income levels is determined by the state of the market.

Secondly, characteristics of economic differentiation within social strata vary with often unpredictable state policy with regard to these strata. By all appearances, fluctuations of economic status within major classes and strata will in the near future depend on the following factors:

- the state of the market, the state of affairs in particular branches and groups of enterprises;
- government policy regarding loss-making enterprises;
- support of concrete social groups by the state; and
- position of trade-unions, political parties and movements.

All these factors will affect the socio-economic differentiation within the social strata of Belarussian society. The political position of concrete socio-professional groups will change according to these fluctuations.

5.4 Regulation of social stratification

Certain correction and modernisation of social structure cannot be avoided in a transitional society. Government control here is a prerequisite. If the present political line of the government remains unchanged in the near future, regulation of stratification process in Belarus is unlikely to be carried out on a large scale and will not break the status quo between major classes and strata. Rather, the government will be periodically redistributing state subvention and manoeuvring between the most active social groups.

Other scenarios are also possible. The fact that about 30% of all Belarussian enterprises are loss-makers and the rigid conditions set by foreign creditors can force the government to accept the idea of inevitability of extensive if not mass unemployment relieved by systems of benefits for the jobless. A step of that kind will affect the interests of a wide range of strata and will force society to relinquish social protests for the generation of a new stereotype whereby unemployment is considered as a 'norm'.

There is one more hypothetical scenario. Certain legislative acts will be adopted and some measures directed at reforms will be taken, such as the most favourable treatment of small and medium-size businesses, privatisation of the service sector, partial land privatisation and so forth. That scenario would boost stratificational changes as well as the formation of a middle class and differentiation of the active population according to the forms of property they possess.

This scenario is possible only under the condition of the active interaction and co-operation of the power structures with the opposition in a combined effort to find a way out of the economic impasse.

Monitoring of the economic and political situation in Belarus would help correct that prognostication.

5

Do 'Russians' Exist as an Ethnic Community?

Viktor Voronkov

I would like to point out beforehand, that in the argument between the primordialists and the situationalists about the meaning of the concept 'ethnic group', I certainly take the side of the majority of sociologists who presume that ethnicity is a socially rather than a biologically based phenomenon. According to that point of view, ethnic groups are formed on the basis of real or imaginary features ascribed to them. Those features serve to discriminate one group from another[1]. In other words, an ethnic group is not a natural category but rather one constructed by human consciousness.

Unfortunately, in Russian ethnosociology there still prevail notions more associated with the colonial ethnography of the 19th century, and which became obsolete in world sociology long ago. Thus, objectivity of existence of ethnos (a notion used solely by Soviet science) has never been doubted until recently. Moreover, the predominant concept of the ethnos is completely racist, since membership of an ethnic group is determined by blood and is fixed by the state in black and white in any document under a special column – 'nationality'. This government policy entailed the formation of a hierarchy of ethnic groups and a respective national policy, in which the 'Russian people' played the role of an 'elder brother' and were considered as 'the first among equals'.[2]

Under conditions of radical societal transformation in which the majority of usual identifications have been destroyed, people begin to look for new communities they would like to join. As post-Soviet society is not yet internally differentiated, ethnic codes acquire special importance.[3] Crisis makes people remember that they belong

---

1 Smelther, N. *Sociology*. Moscow: Fenix, 1994: 306.

2 Russian supremacy was mentioned in a famous toast pronounced by I. Stalin to "the most prominent of all nations of the Soviet Union", to "the leading Russian people". *Bolshevik* 1945, no 10: 1-2.

3 Offe, Claus. *Der Tunnel am Ende des Lichts*. Frankfurt/New York: Campus, 1994: 166-167.

to a certain ethnic group. This fact has proved to be true for the whole population of the CIS, except ... for the Russians living in Russia.

We shall not touch upon issues of the formation of 'ethnic Russians' the genesis of Russian self-consciousness, so much discussed by historians and ethnologists.[4] As far as the state is concerned, Russians are all those who have corresponding registration in the 'nationality' column of their passports. Nationality was determined by the nationality of one's parents, i.e., by 'blood'. The passport system has affected the self-identification of people very profoundly.[5] Considerable assimilation of many ethnic groups was the result of the fact that belonging to the titular nation (Russians) brought many advantages. That was the cause of great differences between the Russians, regarded as such by the state, and those who believed themselves that they were Russians or who were believed to be Russians by others.

A crisis of the pre-existing value system is likely to noticeably affect the national composition of the population of Russia, since many will choose to change the nationality registration in their passports chosen by them before (when such a choice, though limited, was possible). In that connection, many experts predict a decrease of the number of Russians by 10-15 million people in the near future.[6]

Researchers note a weakened and vague character of the national self-consciousness of Russians.[7] In the author's opinion, that is a direct result of the influence exerted on the consciousness of the Russian population by its role as an imperial nation in Russian history, including its Soviet period. The fact that the Russians have never had a mono-ethnic state of their own, combined with the embryonic state of Russian-orientated institutions accounts for the fact that the development of Russian consciousness was largely based on imperial values. The Russian nation as a distinct identity has failed to take shape within the framework of the empire, and after its collapse it has become evident that, but for its imperial aspect, Russian consciousness is a phantom. Some authors doubt, and not without reason, that Russians exist as a separate ethnic group: „Russians as a whole and

---

4 See a survey: Filipov, V.F. „From the history of research on Russian national self-consciousness." *Soviet ethnography* 1991, no. 1: 25 - 33.

5 Dragunskii, D.V. „A forced ethnicity." *Polis* 1993, no. 5: 24-30.

6 Tishkov, V. A. „Strategies and mechanisms of national policy." In *Nationalities Policy in the Russian Federation*. Moscow, 1993: 14.

7 Savoskul, S. „Socio-ethnic problems of Russian people." *Ethnopolis* 1992, no. 1: 94-106.

integral ethnos, as a real community having its own specific and common national consciousness is almost non-existent now"[8] (and it never did exist! – author's note).

The secondary analysis of the conducted surveys shows that the majority of Russians identified themselves as Soviet.[9] The same, however, was characteristic of the majority of representatives of other ethnic groups. Nevertheless, these had a more pronounced ethnic identification (although it was weaker than the Soviet one). As for the Russians, as ethnologists and ethno-sociologists testify, they have, at best, a sub-ethnic, regional identification, or that of *soslovie* [estate] (Petersburgers, Siberians, Notherners, Cossacks and so forth).

Politicians, aiming at revival of 'the great power' and demonstrating by this that the imperial consciousness is still alive, are counting on the 'revival' of Russian self-consciousness. The ex-minister on nationalities S. Shakhrai says: „I want Russian people to feel they are one nation, I want them to remember their origins and roots. Alas, we have got a very short memory on these things. And a possible reason for that is the immaturity of the Russian nation... Russian patriotism and the Russian idea must be held in the focus of attention of politicians at all times".[10] But what are the real prospects for the development of Russian national self-consciousness?

The author is inclined to agree with the opinion of the Russian historian Mikhail Gefter, who said that Russians form a „superethnos which can not be reduced back to an ethnos, to a nation in the common meaning of this word".[11]

A viable Russian nationalism is highly problematic, as it should necessarily include an imperial component, which contradicts the idea of creating a 'Russia of Russians'.[12]

Nevertheless, many participants in this discussion hold the opposite opinion. For many of them, the whole problem of Russians is to get rid of the enemies (esp. internal), who conspire to ruin 'the great Russian nation'. Others are looking for an idea that could unite the whole Russian nation – its existence is not doubted by them, although they do admit that it is currently living through a crisis. The majority of

---

8 Olshanskii, D. „Political psychology of disintegration." *Nezavisimaya gazeta* 16 January 1992.

9 Drobigeva, L.M. „Ethnic self-consciousness of Russians: Ideology and practice." *Soviet ethnography* 1991, no. 1: 5.

10 Shakhrai, S. „We live on a volcano. (Interview)," *Delovaya Zhizn'* 5 March 1994.

11 „Russians at home. A talk between M. Gefter and G. Pavlovskii." In *Burnt by the hearth.* Moscow: Progres, 1990: 277.

12 Dragunskii, D.V. „A forced ethnicity.": 29.

authors, however, try to dodge a precise definition, taking 'Russianism' for granted, as something given and not needing any discussion.

Analysis of the current discussion helps to identify several typical definitions of Russians, which are based on different grounds, that are at the same time considered as fundamental values of cultural revival.

1. *Russians are those who belong to the Orthodox Church.* Let us cite some typical statements of the partisans of this theory. „The Russians do not form a nation or an ethnos, they are a certain mystic unity. The Russian people are the Chosen People, and their national identity is rather a church than an ethnic identity"[13]. „All misfortunes of the Russian people are the result of moving away from Orthodox Christianity. It is evident that it is Orthodox Christianity that has shaped Russian character. The orthodox have been and will remain the core of the Russian nation"[14].

Such definition of Russians narrows to the minimum the circle of those included into the category of 'Russians' according to other criteria. Recent research shows that religiousness of the population and, in particular, the role of Orthodoxy is being evidently exaggerated. Even the collapse of the old system of values did not turn the people to the Orthodox Church. Instead, all kinds of sects, quasi-religious organizations and parascientific notions have developed widely.

The Orthodox Church, despite the obvious state protectionism, is unlikely to realize its ambitions for the following reasons: firstly, the Soviet regime successfully eradicated the religious feelings of the majority of Russia's population; secondly, the Orthodox Church has discredited itself over the last decades[15], and thirdly, Orthodox Christianity, which is often vulgarized by the remains of paganism in the people's consciousness, has many interpretations. Moreover, a number of Russian nationalist organizations declared Slavic paganism as the true Russian religion, regarding

---

13 Dughin, A.G. „Russians - ethnos or nation?" *Kentavr* 1993, no. 2: 40-41.

14 Saltykov, A. „Archpriest. Russian Orthodoxy and the spiritual revival of the nation." *Kentavr* 1993, no. 2: 39-40. It is very characteristic of the Church not to discriminate between Russian and orthodox, that fact was noticed by a Soviet poet B.Slutskii in his unpublished poem *Jewish Priest*: "Promptly baptized, without bureaucracy, He stood up, people's resentments washed off. A Jew, he remained for a minister, But a Russian he became for the metropolitan".

15 A typical anecdote can serve as an illustration of the attitude to the Church in the former USSR: "At a service in a church. The priest is approached by the sextan, and the latter whispers into his ear: "Finish the service, father, we are late for the party gathering!"

Orthodoxy as a 'Jewish' means of enslavement and genocide of the Russian people[16].

2. *Russians are those who have specific qualities, the bearers of the 'Russian idea'*. A similar quasi-religious reason accounts for the definition of Russians as a Messianic nation chosen by God, as a bearer of a certain 'Russian idea' formulated in many different ways by those who take part in the current public discussion. However, the irrational character of the notions that the apologists of the 'Russian idea' resort to makes any objective research impossible. They cite all kinds of myths concerning the Russian national character, such as 'an innate feeling of social justice', a 'universal compassion', 'supreme morality', 'life according to the conscience' and so forth. One author generalizes: „A specifically Russian community has absorbed the idea of the priority of mind over matter and a strong feeling of justice offsetting egoism“[17].

Our research gives us grounds to put forward a hypothesis that the 'Russian idea' is a subject of debates in a very narrow circle of intelligentsia and does not concern the self-consciousness of all Russians in general. As for the 'Russian national character', it appears that taking into account the complexity and vagueness of this notion, a historical, changing character of that idea should be empirically demonstrated (of course, it would be more correct to speak about the character of an inhabitant of Russia, i.e., about a product of certain historical conditions, which is usually *homo sovieticus* called in social and political journalism – if we are to take into account that the character of a Russian of today has been formed exclusively by the Soviet conditions of the last decades, regardless of his or her ethnic origin in the majority of cases). In that connection, research into the current radical transformation of the 'national character' and into the crisis of 'mentalities' as well as into the formation of new behavioural patterns promises to be most interesting.

3. *A Russian is, in the 1st place, a representative of the state*[18]. Authors sharing that opinion evade endless discussions about separating Russians from the rest of the people living in Russia, and they do not try to define Russians as an ethnic and cultural group. They use the word 'Russian' as an adjective (a Russian Jew, a Russian Georgian, a Russian Russian) denoting an inhabitant of Russia or a citizen

---

16 See, for instance: Zarikov, S. „When the stars fall.“ *K Toporu* 1993, no. 5; also Evola, V. *Pagan imperialism*. Moscow: Russkoe slovo, 1992.

17 Kulkov, V.M. „Russian idiosyncrasy: Global experience and economic reform.“ *Vestnik Moskovskogo Universiteta* Series 6 (1993), no 4: 61.

18 Hohryakov, G. „Russians, who are we?“ Moscow: B. i., 1993: 32.

of the Russian State. Incidentally, in foreign languages two Russian words: 'russkii' – Russian, and 'rossiiskii' – of Russia, are both translated as 'Russian' (if a person is from Russia, then he or she is Russian). That is why all Russian-speaking emigrants from Russia, regardless of the ethnic group they belong to, are indiscriminately called Russians.

4. *Russians are those who were brought up in the Russian cultural environment, for whom Russian is their native language*. Everyone who speaks and thinks in Russian is Russian, regardless of the nationality indicated in his passport[19] (note: the word 'nationality' in Soviet parlance refers not to the State but to the particular national groups that compose it). That liberal definition is a widespread one, underlining that ethnic identification is a matter of conscious choice for every citizen.

5. *Russians are those who have Russian blood in their veins.* That racist position is characteristic of the majority of Russian nationalists, who treat membership of a certain ethnic group in terms of biology, as something innate and genetically determined. However, since Russians living on immense territories mixed over many centuries with the indigenous population of those territories, there is no single ethnic type of Russian, and thus to talk about the purity of blood is meaningless. Nevertheless, the programme of a movement called *Russian National Unity* reads: „one of the main concerns of the future National State will be protection of genetic purity of the Russian Nation...„[20]

No matter how much we doubt the existence of a Russian ethnic community, we must admit that some territorial communities have emerged over the last years and that their ethnic self-identification has become much more pronounced after the collapse of the USSR, so that now they suit the concept of a separate ethnic group more than ever. We speak about a certain part of those 25 million of 'Russian-speaking' people, who against their will found themselves trapped outside Russia in the newly independent States, the former Soviet republics. Those communities are being formed under the influence of a real or alleged ethnic discrimination that they are subject to in those states. Just as 'Jews exist due to anti-Semitism', the Russians owe their national identity to what the right wing calls 'russophobia'. One researcher

---

19 Ushakov, B. „A great nation." *Nezavisimaya Gazeta* 3 June 1994.
20 *Russkii poryadok*, no. 9-1, 1993-1994.

rightly says: „Our society is a multinational one, and a feeling of Russian national unity can be kindled only through strong ethnic tension.“[21]

The complexity of the problem of what should be included into the concept of 'Russian', and the futility of any discussion on that subject, call on researchers to put an end to „one more genetic feature of post-Soviet sociology, namely what is called 'expert journalism' which gives comments instead of fulfilling the main task of scientific research – to find new knowledge and to conduct primary research, and only after that to build theoretical constructions“.[22]

Unfortunately, all sociological research known to the author was based on mass public polls, which do not even slightly clarify the problem, on the contrary, they create a certain artefact. While we shall not allow ourselves to be drawn into the debate about the possibility of applying quantitative methods to sociology, we should, however, acknowledge that such a delicate problem as ethnic identification requires adequate methods of research.

To the author's mind, we should put aside traditional attempts to precisely determine the content of the concept of 'Russian'. It would be much more original to try to locate the confines of the community that identifies itself and is identified by others as 'the Russians', and only after that could we try to find out how its characteristics are related to its boundaries and its values.

The theory of ethnic boundaries is a recent one[23], and it has never been applied in Russia to concrete research. At the same time, this theory has considerably explanatory capacity, especially in cases of mutual penetration of cultures and indistinct ethnic boundaries. In the case of Russians, that theory seems to be the only instrument that can help to reliably identify the community in question. Identification of community boundaries through the identification and self-identification of the subjects belonging to it, helps to understand how those boundaries are strengthened from within and from beyond, and what processes are taking place on the boundaries themselves.

The very first research on the formation of the Russian community in Estonia and a certain amount of circumstantial evidence from other countries of the CIS, have unexpectedly brought to light the fact that the ethnic factor does not play such an

---

21 Belov, G.A. „About national interest and the 'Russian idea'.“ *Vestnik Moskovskogo Universiteta* Series 12 (1993), no. 5: 69.

22 Barth Fredrik (ed.). *Ethnic Groups and Boundaries. The Social Organization of Culture Difference*. Bergen-Oslo: Universitetsforlaget, 1969.

23 Barth Fredrik (ed.). *Ethnic Groups and Boundaries. The Social Organization of Culture Difference*. Bergen-Oslo: Universitetsforlaget, 1969.

important role for the Russians living there as is ascribed to it in the political arena. Moreover, as people adapt to new conditions, their ethnic peculiarities quickly lose their significance. As for the young, they are not familiar with that problem at all. Their ethnic identification is so weak that there appeared a range of newly created subethnic groups (Russian Estonians, Estonian Russians, people who are neither Estonians nor Russians, Europeans, citizen of the world).

The Russian community in Estonia is being built so far by the efforts of politicians and the older generation. Significantly, it has become clear that the majority of Russians living in the countries of the CIS do not identify themselves with the Russians living in Russia (which was also characteristic of Russian communities in the Baltic States in 1920-1940). Thus it would be unjustified to consider all 25 million of Russians living outside Russia as a part of the Russian community.

The author advances the hypothesis that because of the historical conditions of Russia's development, 'ethnic Russians' do not exist as one community, which is subject to idealization, for example, by the Russian nationalists, who consider it to be their social base. „Russians are a certain polyethnic or a superethnic community, which can be defined only negatively, i.e., these are all those who live in Russia, excluding those who identify themselves as belonging to other ethnic groups".

It has already been mentioned that this community with its indistinct boundaries is very unstable. Millions of Russians living outside Russia no longer consider themselves to be 'Russians of Russia'. One can suppose that since a regional or a subethnic identity for the Russians is much more important than an ethnic identity, the imaginary community in question is a nominal one and is much less consolidated than is asserted in the public discussion taking place now in Russian society. Economic stimuli of regionalism and the opposition of local and central elites closely conform to the regional identity preferred by the people of Russia, which strengthens the tendency of the further disintegration of the empire.[24]

Russian nationalism has as its basis a fundamental idea of existence (or creation, or revival) of a Russian *national state*, which is organized according to the 'rules of the game' that Russians are accustomed to, that is the rules conforming with their cultural traditions. A certain percentage of non-Russians in the population does not

---

24 It is worth noting that every new crisis of society arouses separatism. It is not by chance that a discussion on autonomy of St.Petersburg, very popular in 1991 with the local mass media, has been kindled again during the war in Chechnya under a more radical slogan of a 'free city of St. Petersburg'.

prevent the implementation of the national principle, unless those non-Russians break the 'rules of the game'. The difference when comparing European national states with the idea of the creation of a similar one in Russia arises not from the principle as such, but from the likelihood of such a state in Russia. Since Russia existed until recently as an empire, it would be hard to expect a prompt change of cultural stereotypes connected with an imperial consciousness. That is why it is not yet clear whether certain nations in Russia which occupy their own territories and have a certain degree of self-government will agree to voluntarily join the Russian national state or will continue their struggle for independence, for their own national 'rules of the game'.

Formally, there are three ways of forming the Russian nation. The first is to 'let go' all those who do not want to live by the rules formulated in the Centre, to stop being an empire and to form the Russian nation from the citizens of a new state. This variant is unlikely, as is shown by the contemporary political process, which reveals unremitting imperial ambitions of Russian politicians.

The second way is to try to proceed with the imperial policy and form one integral Russian nation by means of force. Theoretically, this variant is possible, provided there is enough time for it, but practically speaking, it is a utopia. The war in Chechnya is just more proof that preservation of a polyethnic state in the form of an empire has no future.

The third way, and the most likely one, no matter how paradoxical it may sound, is to 'resign oneself' to one's ethnic 'deficiencies'. In this case, we will have a non-ethnic state that will include ethnic minorities. In this way Russians will become citizens of Russia without particular ethnic attributes and together with other inhabitants of Russia, who will want to retain their ethnic self-identification, they will form one nation. Thus, the lack of 'additional ethnic attributes' that was formerly thought to be a defect of Russians will now turn into an advantage and will mean that they will have no 'additional troubles'. Consensus in such a state emerges out of the fact that ethnic Russians do not need those 'additional ethnic attributes', (for their numbers are too great) to realize elements of their ethnic culture, whereas non-Russian Russians need both those 'additional attributes' and a corresponding degree of 'autonomy' to do so.

It must be noted that almost all researchers share the opinion that, despite the many contradictions of Soviet nationalities policy, there formed a rather solid supra-ethnic community – the 'Soviet people'. It can even be regarded as a nation (or co-citizenship) in the European sense, and at the same time, as a socio-cultural community, the nucleus of which is constituted by the semi-mythical 'ethnic Russians'. If that part of the 'Soviet people' who happened to be on the territory of Russia after the collapse of the USSR had retained their unity, then formation of the Russian nation would have been a much easier problem. But an almost total denouncement of all former ideological values and destruction of the Soviet identity hinder the formation of the Russian nation on the territory of Russia now.

6

Self-Help Initiatives:

Forces of Self-Healing within Russian Society?

Frank Fabel

In the following text the author relies on two years of work-experience with self-help initiatives in St.Petersburg. Since 1992 he has been working in the St.Petersburg office of the organisation *German-Russian Exchange*, which was founded in that year with the aim of supporting socially engaged initiatives in Russia, thereby furthering democratisation prospects. Opened in November 1992 at a central location on Nevskii Prospekt, the office has since been run continuously by German and Russian staff and is financed exclusively by donations and project-funding. The office is a focus for self-help initiatives in St.Petersburg as well as social workers and sociologists, journalists and deputies from the entire north-western region, youth organisations and travellers interested in social affairs. The address register contains more than 4000 contacts and there are profiles and short descriptions of all well-known organisations and self-help initiatives for the following problem areas: care for the elderly, work with children and young people, handicap and chronic illness, health care and legal support for drug addicts, army personnel, the homeless and politically repressed, women's organisations, environmental groups and the unemployed. The German-Russian Exchange publishes selections of these profiles of self-help initiatives in German-Russian booklets; so far five booklets have been edited on different topics. A quarterly newsletter is published in German, as well as a small Russian bulletin, focusing on legal questions. The organisation finances the publication of the newspaper *Na dne*, which is partly distributed by homeless people and covers social topics. A small library (including a subject-catalogue) has been put together which specialises in law, human rights and social sciences. Elementary books have been partly translated by the German-Russian Exchange. The office not only provides contacts with the West, but also links together people with the same concerns within Russia, from the grass roots level to high-ranking institutions. The office also provides room for seminars addressing such basics as organisational development and management, public relations and bookkeeping, as well as highly specialised seminars on legal support concerning, for example, the situation in prisons and the situation of drug addicts.

1 Some Concrete Examples of Self-Help Initiatives in Russia Today

Are self-help initiatives, associations for mutual help, and grass roots organisations a sensible and effective regulator within Russian society today? Why are self-help initiatives functioning in Russia and how are they functioning? How effective are they in themselves and also in relation to other forces? Are they the widely hoped-for partners for stability and democratisation?

We present four typical self-help initiatives, the experience of which will be described below: the homeless-initiative *Nochlezhka* (Night Shelter), the self-help group for drug addicts *Vozvrashchenie* (Return), the human rights association *Grazhdanskii Kontrol'* (Citizens' Control) and *Soldatskie Materi* (Soldiers' Mothers). These profiles help to define and question the notion of 'self-help' in Russia. Subsequently, the effect of the self-help movement shall be roughly estimated as to the concrete impact it has on the social system. Furthermore, the importance of this movement for society and its function within society shall be put in relation to other 'forces of order'.

1.1 Vozvrashchenie

Dmitrii Ostrovskii, who himself used to be addicted to opiates and underwent forced abstinence in a penal colony – the former *'narkozona'* – learnt (after his release) from travelling Americans that in the US there exist associations for former drug addicts. This was what inspired him to create *Vozvrashchenie* (Return). Dmitrii Ostrovskii founded the association and put an end to his career as a diver and high-rise worker in order to dedicate himself to the care of drug addicts who were willing to quit using drugs. A stable group of co-workers emerged and today the inner circle consists of about 20 former addicts who help on a regular basis. The joint relapse of a large part of the group has left deep impressions on *Vozvrashchenie:* the organisation now only offers physical withdrawal in small groups. Experience with government institutions, be it the militia or state-hospitals for drug therapy, have marked the relations of *Vozvrashchenie* with official bodies over a long period of time: the group worked in hiding and avoided public attention. Official institutions were met with suspicion. The group has a religious orientation, and all of its members and recent addicts gather strength in the monastery of Pechory near Pskov where the group has converted its own *dacha*. With the help of an army base whose commander claims that he quit his drug addiction with the help of *Vozvrashchenie*, the group was able to start the first therapy centre: nobody suspected that the first Russian non-governmental therapy centre was located in a closed military zone. Today it houses a carpentry workshop where former addicts find stability after the therapy and which should provide *Vozvrashchenie* with financial support. Six members work as paid staff for *Vozvrashchenie* at present. Thanks to German and French donations and the dedicated work of the circle of friends, the group was able to build their own three-storied house, a therapy centre in Vsevolozhk. A mobile information facility – a converted ambulance, bought by donations from the charity of the German Lutheran church in Berlin – serves drug addicts at particular social 'hot-spots' with medical help and advice. Although the organisation's material basis is wide and solid, there is no backing for running costs. Apart from their therapy work, the group has no political ambitions and strongly fights, for example, attempts to legalise hard and soft drugs – an agenda put forward in Russia by the Radical Party. The introduction of a methadone and substitution programme in Russia is one of the primary future objectives of *Vozvrashchenie*.

1.2 Nochlezhka

Valerii Sokolov evaded military service, thereby losing his *'propiska'*, i.e., his residence permit, which, according to the former Soviet passport laws, rendered him a person without fixed abode. For some time he lived in the Caucasus and himself experienced the life of a vagrant. In 1989 he founded *Nochlezhka* (Night Shelter) in St.Petersburg. Then it was little more than a hopeful name, an occupied cellar at Pushkinskaya Ulitsa 10 and a handful of co-workers. As the city government proved unable to pass on coupons to the homeless during the food-crisis in 1990/91, the recently founded *Nochlezhka* took over this task. Cheques for privatisation, the so-called privatisation-vouchers, were also distributed by *Nochlezhka* and the homeless were registered through the group. Still illegal, the organisation was given official tasks by the city government! Imagine, for purposes of comparison, that the squatters in the Hamburg Hafenstraße were officially entrusted by the city's senate to distribute identification papers and social benefits! Thanks to financial donations from Germany, *Nochlezhka* was able to open a soup-kitchen in January 1993. For two years the kitchen has been providing for initially for 300, then for 600 homeless every day. *Nochlezhka* also offers legal advice for the homeless while the clothes store provides them with clothes donations. Since its establishment, *Nochlezhka* has not only been pursuing humanitarian aims: the work should be accompanied by corresponding research, it being clear to the initiators that homelessness in Russia is not only a social, but also a political problem. The organisation is of the opinion that the law is making people homeless and deliberately obstructing their reintegration. Therefore *Nochlezhka* also concentrates on political activity. A digest was published on various social problem areas. For six months now the newspaper *Na dne* has been in circulation (distributed by the homeless).

Nochlezhka also organised a polling-station during the parliamentary elections in 1993, where votes could be handed in by those not registered in St.Petersburg. Thanks to the influence of *Nochlezhka,* the candidate Yulii Andreevich Rybakov – a friend of Sergei Kovalev – was voted into the State Duma. Rybakov himself met and developed a respect for the organisation's founder in the dissidents' coffee-house *Saigon.* Rybakov has subsequently put the representation of human rights for marginals such as drug addicts and homeless on his agenda.

Nochlezhka today is very influential, but has no economic basis.

1.3 Grazhdanskii Kontrol

During his student years, Boris Pustyntsev protested against the Soviet occupation of Hungary. In 1962 he was released from imprisonment and made his living by translating, working as a literary editor and as a synchronization supervisor in the *Lenfilm*-studios. Pustyntsev is one of the founding members of the group *Memorial* (association for the politically repressed) in St.Petersburg; within the St. Petersburg group he heads the department for human rights. In order not to endanger *Memorial,* as he says, he initiated the foundation of the public association *Grazhdanskii Kontrol'.* The organisation has made it their aim to control the activities of the secret services and to defend civilians from the all-powerful special services. Pustyntsev himself was beaten up by strangers in front of his apartment and now suffers from impaired sight as a result. *Grazhdanskii Kontrol'* has only ten members, among them the well-known lawyer Yurii Schmidt, who is also chairman of the committee 'Advocates for Human Rights', Yurii Vdovin, the former chairman of the committee for *glasnost'* and mass media in the 'Petrosoviet', and Sergei Khakhaev, board member of *Memorial,* St.Petersburg. *Grazhdanskii Kontrol'* organises international seminars, works out legal proposals and tries to promote them. The organisation has extensive national and international contacts. On a parliamentary level it maintains work-contacts with the commission of the German Bundestag concerning misuse of power in the GDR. Even though the organisation has sprung from direct, personal concern, it does not as yet offer any special services and support for those in need. Therefore it has no specific social basis.

1.4 Soldatskie Materi

Ella Polyakova, the heart of the *Soldatskie Materi* (Soldiers' Mothers) organisation in St.Petersburg comes from an officer's family. She was motivated, however, not by repressions against her children, but by concern for the Army, its internal deterioration and corruption. From this protective and distanced point of view, she shows an understanding for the worries and desperation of parents whose children die during their Army service or are abused there. She was first moved to action by the Army being sent to the Baltics in 1991, where for the first time Army detachments where brought in to settle internal conflicts. At the height of the conflict she travelled to Riga with her family.

With high stakes and great personal risk, *Soldatskie Materi* has mobilised the only publicly visible protest against the war in Chechnya. Public attention has focused on these actions, on the picket lines in front of the Ministry of Defence, but *Soldatskie Materi* has long since been working at the grass roots level: the organisation provides consultations for young soldiers who suffer from abuse by their elders, whose health problems are not acknowledged by the Army doctors or who refuse to serve in the Army. Even before the Chechnya crisis, lawyers of *Soldatskie Materi* assisted more than 400 persons per month seeking advice. *Soldatskie Materi* also provides support for parents worried about their sons in the Army. The St.Petersburg branch of *Soldatskie Materi,* founded in 1992, numbers 50 members; 15 people work in the co-ordinating committee, the leading body. *Soldatskie Materi* works entirely on a voluntary basis. Besides *Soldatskie Materi* there is also the association *Soldatskaya Mat'* (Soldier's Mother) which works more to preserve the memory of deceased conscripts and also offers consultations at the *Dom Ofitserov* (Officers' House).

2 Self-Help Initiatives: Margin and Centre of Russian Society

We have presented a biographical sketch of four organisations which are still marked by Soviet history. Pressure on the homeless, drug-addicts, young conscripts and dissidents, all of whom have their counterparts in Western marginal groups, furthered the creation of self-help initiatives. Nevertheless, our Western concept of marginals as a fertile ground for self-help initiatives is too narrow. The Western concept is based on a functioning democratic society, which, by functioning, excludes certain groups. In a non-functioning society such as that of Russia, in the absence of a stabilising centre the majority itself is marginalised. This we experience when we repeatedly hear the complaint that the West is helping 'those', but not us 'normal people'. Specialised Western help for marginal groups is met with incomprehension by the degraded Soviet middle-class. Strangely enough, as we will show further on, these Western concepts for marginals unwittingly affect the centre of the post-Soviet power structure.

Nowadays, marginalization through Soviet law has virtually come to a halt, while marginalization through the functioning market has only just begun. Self-help initiatives fill this historical gap much more than is thought possible in the West. The self-help movement reaches far into women's and youth politics and it makes sense to look at these political areas under the overall concept of self-help.

We prefer the concept of self-help in these atypical areas to the internationally used acronym NGO (non-governmental organisation). NGO is a negative concept defined by what an organisation is not: governmental and commercial. The author, however, holds that the self-constituting element, the art of self-discovery, is the decisive criteria for effective co-operation.

The preceding organisational biographies have shown that circles of people concerned with a mutual problem can very quickly develop into professional pressure groups. Non-professionalism or volunteerism do not seem to us to be fitting criteria for the identification of self-help initiatives. On the contrary, a rapid development of professionalism should be very welcome since self-help initiatives fulfil a much wider spectrum of functions than in the West.

3 The Functions of Self-Help Initiatives within Russian Society

Self-help initiatives realise a number of concrete social tasks in Russia. Which tasks, however, do they realise within the context of society? Why are self-help groups – we can say this outright – so successful in Russia?

- Self-help initiatives satisfy a need for solidarity and security. The link is often much closer than in Western self-help initiatives, which come into being and are again dissolved, which are meant to cope with transitional, individual problem situations. Where Russian self-help initiatives are concerned, one is tempted to speak of 'fatal communities'. This applies in particular to self-help initiatives of chronically ill people, who hardly find care and support outside the group (for example *ASSKOL* – the association of colostomy patients, *ALLERGIK* for patients with allergic and respiratory diseases, *PAPBM* for those with mucoviscidosis, and others). The above mentioned initiatives – *Nochlezhka, Vozvrashchenie, Grazhdanskii Kontrol'* and *Soldatskie Materi* play an essential part – if not *the* essential part – in the lives of their clients.

- Self-help initiatives function in an area which has never been occupied by the state or other charity organisations. Advice and representation of the interests of their clients at a trial or before the administration are such entirely new concepts that self-help initiatives enjoy almost total freedom of action. For example, the shelter for homeless girls *Evfimiya* was founded as a closed-type joint-stock company. As the establishment of the shelter lacked legal basis, the taking-in of the homeless was bordering on kidnapping. The administration had to choose between closing the shelter or including *Evfimiya* in the process of licensing. Thereby *Evfimiya* won agenda-setting powers, but only in the short run. *Evfimiya* was shut down in February 1995 for reasons of hygiene.
- Self-help initiatives offer themselves as partners for Western aid. The fact that there is something to distribute significantly highlights the attraction of self-help initiatives, even in comparison to the administration, since they have nothing to distribute. Nevertheless, self-help initiatives usually start working without money. Funding at the right time rather furthers the development of professionalism.

These three sources of strength for self-help groups taken together – solidarity, freedom of action and Western support – characterise the dynamics of the present self-help movement. These dynamics are so powerful, that again and again essential parts of the inner organisational mechanism of self-help initiatives overheat. The self-help initiatives develop their own ideology, their own hardened leadership structures. The success of self-help initiatives is closely dependent on the '*hetmen*', the founding-fathers and the focal points within the group. Many of these people have ruined their health as a representative of a good cause. This should also hint at the fact that self-help initiatives – despite being vehicles of the democratisation process – are not necessarily organised on democratic principles.

4 The Influence of Self-Help Initiatives

How effective are self-help initiatives? Self-help activists often ask themselves this question with a note of depression. The bog in which Russian society has become stuck seems too deep, problems seem unsolvable. But are there any objective means of evaluation? On the whole, more than 3000 public organisations are registered in St.Petersburg, pursuing more or less social aims. About one-tenth of them conducts serious work. In terms of quantity, the achievements of self-help initiatives in St.Petersburg are impressive. Some examples: For two years *Nochlezhka* has been offering soup for free. 600 portions are handed out every day. With the help of a voucher system, 1800 persons are reached – hot soup every third day. More than 11,000 homeless have been registered to date and have been provided with a service of some sort.

Annually *Vozvrashchenie* reaches 140 drug addicts willing to undergo therapy and aims to double its capacity in 1995. Other drug initiatives, such as the parent-association *Azariya* or the brotherhood *Novye Palomniki* are working more in the field of education and consultation and thus reach a larger number of clients.

ASSKOL, the association of colostomy patients, has been catering for three years to about 1000 patients with cancer of the colon, providing them with medical aid.

Memorial, the association for the politically repressed, numbers 2700 members in St.Petersburg to date. The work of *Memorial* includes the organisation of cultural evenings, support at trials and care through the *Memorial* pharmacy.

In terms of quantity, the self-help initiatives are reaching a large part of the population in social crisis situations. A darker picture is to be found where standard risks are concerned: old age, accidents, illness, unemployment, death. *Memorial* has partly taken over the roll of a deposit-bank in case of death, from which donations are given for funerals. For certain chronic diseases there are self-help initiatives, also for the unemployed of certain professional groups (the group of unemployed mathematicians, for example). The standard risk of old age has barely been touched by self-help initiatives. We know of only two spontaneously formed circles of pensioners which exist independently of governmental organisations. The inefficiencies of governmental care for the aged are a huge challenge for self-help initiatives.

The author is convinced, however, that self-help initiatives are not a substitute for ailing state social services, even if self-help initiatives have in fact taken over large parts of government tasks. Self-help initiatives do not only fulfil tasks in the various social niches – their strength lies more in their unwanted socio-political role, where self-help initiatives carry the social agenda into politics. Unwanted, because everything to do with politics has become deeply discredited in Russia. Even if self-help initiatives convey an atmosphere of comfort and instinctively deny official politics, they are in fact the agents of politisation and democratic permeation. The fact that separate groups represent monarchist or strict religious positions are in this case no contradiction.

Self-help initiatives are rather like an escalator, bringing to light things which had been hidden underground; they are the transmission belts in the process of creating representation in society.

Nochlezhka, as has already been mentioned, has its own access to the Duma. After four successful years, *Vozvrashchenie* was invited to the 'Co-ordinating Committee in the Fight against Drug Addiction and the Drug Trade'. For the first time, representatives of the security forces spoke with former drug addicts and representatives of the city administration have even promised support. All four initiatives are prominent in the public arena. Hardly a day passes without newspapers in St.Petersburg reporting about one of these groups. Via these various channels, formerly taboo subjects – in this case homelessness, drug addiction, conscripts and the repressed – are made public.

However, the paths into the sphere of public balance of interests are naturally individual ones. All attempts at gathering together the lobby-work of social initiatives have so far failed. The president initiated the creation of chambers for the public at the beginning of 1994 which are supposed to represent social initiatives at both municipal and federal level, thereby legitimising the government. In St.Petersburg over 250 public organisations gathered by invitation from the mayor's office. While the public chamber in Moscow tried to constitute itself independently from the administration and elected an executive office with thirteen members, its St. Petersburg counterpart has as yet failed to acquire independent status. *Memorial* and *Soldatskie Materi* have refused to take part.

Besides this initiative from above to gather together social groups, there are attempts from below to merge the political and social sphere, to create a representation inside the executive powers, which themselves so desperately need a social basis.

7

Interethnic Relations and Ethnic Tolerance in Ukraine

An In-Depth Analytical Report

Natal'ya Panina

The transition from isolationist (territorial, social, and mental) principles of social system functioning to principles of openness and co-operation is one of the most important preconditions of transforming a closed (traditional-communitarian or totalitarian) society into an open democratic society[1].

A certain level of tolerance towards members of various social groups, to which an individual does not belong, is a psychological basis of any social partnership.

In a situation of heightened social tension (caused by an economic slump and a struggle of different political forces for power), tolerance of members of one ethnic group towards other ethnic groups is regarded as a most important factor, if not of societal stabilization then, at least of prevention of civil war or murderous interethnic clashes, which a number of republics of the FSU (Azerbaidzhan, Armenia, Georgia, Moldova, Tadzhikistan, Kirgizstan, Uzbekistan, the Ossetiyan-Ingushetian conflict in Russia) failed to avoid.

Numerous sociological polls, conducted by the central Ukrainian branch of the All-Union Centre for Public Opinion Research and the Institute for Sociology with Ukraine's National Academy of Sciences in 1989-1991, included some questions which touched, to a varying degree, upon problems of interethnic relations. The data obtained did not reveal any widespread pronounced nationalist attitudes among the population of most regions of Ukraine. Despite this, however, and despite the absence of outbursts of interethnic strife in Ukraine, public opinion polls typically register a high level of anxiety among the population about the possibility of interethnic conflict: in all the polls on issues of utmost concern for the population, the problem of likely interethnic feuds figured most prominently among stress-causing factors.

---

1 Popper, K. *Otkrytoe obshchestvo i ego vragi* [Open Society and Its Enemies]. Moskva: Kulturnaya Initsiativa, 1992. Vols. 1&2.

The peak of concern about possible interethnic conflicts was registered in 1992, when almost half of Ukraine's adult population (49%) named the possibility of interethnic conflicts as one of the major problems they were most apprehensive of. At the same time, the share of people who found themselves involved in conflicts triggered by disrespect for national/ethnic dignity, remained at the same level (about 3%). Discrepancies between the extent of personal experience of interethnic confrontation and the growth of concern about possible interethnic conflict seem to be explained, first and foremost, by outbreaks of interethnic strife in other regions of the former Soviet Union rather than by the way interethnic conflicts developed in Ukraine and policies pursued by the leadership with regard to ethnic groups. However, in order to prognosticate possible paths of development of interethnic relations in Ukraine and, most importantly, to be able to spot in advance probable factors of heightened interethnic tensions, one should have much more evidence than some fragmentary data obtained in response to a few individual questions, included, as a rule, into prompt topical public opinion polls on the most urgent problems.

1 Ethnic Tolerance Measuring Procedure

An in-depth analysis of the problem presupposes special methods which make it possible to measure the level of general ethnic/national tolerance as an underlying psychological basis of interethnic behaviour. One of such methods is Bogardus' social distance[2]. It allows the measurement of a person's social attitude towards members of other ethnic groups and nationalities – a certain psychological predisposition to affiliate with or, conversely, to alienate from other ethnic groups or nationalities, irrespective of their personal qualities and peculiarities[3]. A respondent's answer to the question of the capacity in which he/she is ready to accept representatives of other ethnic groups or nationalities makes it possible to

2 Park, R.E. „The Concept of Social Distance." *Journal of Applied Sociology* 8 (1924): 339-344; Bogardus, E.S. „Measuring Social Distance." *Journal of Applied Sociology* 9 (1925): 299-308.

3 For applications of this method in ethnosociological research, see Ktsoyeva, G.U. „Metody izucheniya etnicheskikh stereotipov" [Methods of Studying Ethnic Stereotypes]. In *Sotsialnaya Psikhologiya i Obshchestvennaya Praktika* [Social Psychology and Social Practice] 1985: 225-231; Koltsov, V.B. „Sotsialnaya distantsiya v mezhnatsionalnom obshchenii: opyt postroyeniya integralnogo pokazatelya [Social Distance in Interethnic Communication: An Attempt to Devise an Integral Index]." *Sotsiologhicheskiye Issledovaniya* [Sociological Studies] 2 (1989): 26-29; Pantic, D. „Nacionalna Distanca Gradana Jugoslavije." In *Jugoslavija na kriznoj prekpetnici*. Beograd: IDNCPIJM (1991): 168-186.

determine a measure of social distance he/she would prefer to be preserved between herself or himself and the group in question.

The scale is organized on a cumulative principle, which allows one to determine the index (in points) of social distance vis-à-vis a certain ethnic group or nationality: „ready to accept them as members of the family“ – one point, „as a close friend“ – two points. „as a neighbour“ – three points. „as a fellow-worker“ – four points, „as a resident of the country“ – five points, „as a tourist/visitor“ – six points, „I would not admit them to Ukraine at all“ – seven points. Thus, one point signifies maximum tolerance, while seven points signifies extreme intolerance.

Using a list of 23 nationalities, the authors applied the Bogardus social distance scale in two studies (in Kiev in August 1990 and in July 1991), the outcomes of which confirmed the reliability of the information obtained by means of this method[4].

A special study of ethnic tolerance of Ukraine's population was undertaken in April 1992 and in May 1994 using the Bogardus scale. The two studies used a national sample of Ukraine's adult population (over 18 years old; the calculated sample size was 1800 people, representative of regions [*oblasts*] of residence), types of settlement (town/village), nationality/ethnic group and educational level of Ukraine's adult population as a whole.

The list of ethnic groups/nationalities, presented to respondents for evaluation in April 1992, included 16 groups: Ukrainians, Russians, Belarussians, Jews, a number of nationalities of the former USSR republics, Western and Eastern European, Asian and African countries, as well as Ukrainians living abroad (expatriates in the Ukrainian diaspora).

In May 1994 the list was somewhat modified by excluding a number of ethnic groups/nationalities which were of no political interest for the monitoring of attitudes and including some nationalities/ethnic groups living along Ukraine's borders whose attitudes were of practical interest for political decision-making purposes – namely Moldavians, Serbians, Turks and Slovaks.

---

4 Golovakha, E. and N. Panina „Interethnic Relations and Ethnic Tolerance in Ukraine.“ *Jews ans Jewish Topics in the Soviet Union and Eastern Europe*. 14 (1991): 27-30; Golovakha, E.I., N.V. Panina, and N.N. Churilov. *Kiev 1990-1991. Sotsiologhicheskiye Reportazhi* [Kiev 1990-1991: Sociological Reports]. Kiev: Naukova Dumka (1992), 129 pp.

2 Attitudes of Ukraine's Population towards Various Nationalities/Ethnic Groups

Attitudes of Ukraine's adult population towards members of various ethnic groups/nationalities in 1992 (i.e., half a year after Ukraine became an independent state) can generally be characterized as being orientated towards national/ethnic isolation (Table 1):

Table 1 *Social distance vis-à-vis various ethnic groups/nationalities as evaluated by Ukraine's population (April 1992): „I agree to accept members of the given ethnic group/nationality as..." 1: members of my family; 2: close friends; 3: neighbours; 4: colleagues at work; 5: inhabitants of Ukraine; 6: visitors of Ukraine; 7: I would not allow them into Ukraine at all*

Level of Tolerance	*1*	*2*	*3*	*4*	*5*	*6*	*7*	Index
Ukrainians	79	9	3	1	7	2	0	1.55
Russians	43	24	10	3	11	7	2	2.46
Belarussians	29	27	14	4	13	12	1	2.85
Ukrainian expatriates	24	22	7	4	18	23	2	3.48
Poles	15	22	14	4	12	28	5	3.77
Jews	10	14	15	11	23	18	10	4.18
Hungarians	9	14	17	5	15	35	4	4.24
Americans	11	13	9	15	10	38	4	4.31
Germans	8	13	9	16	12	37	5	4.43
French	9	13	8	13	11	41	4	4.45
Romanians	8	12	13	6	14	38	8	4.56
Japanese	4	11	9	19	9	43	4	4.66
Crimean Tatars	3	6	9	5	31	29	17	5.09
Georgians	3	8	9	5	16	34	26	5.26
Vietnamese	2	7	6	9	10	52	14	5.29
Arabs	3	6	5	7	11	51	17	5.37
Negroes	2	6	5	6	11	50	20	5.49
Gypsies	3	4	7	3	22	26	35	5.55

(% of all those polled; N = 1752)

The data obtained made it possible to answer one question raised as a result of previous research, i.e., why, despite a generally favourable situation in the sphere of interethnic relations, a considerable part of the population is still fearful of interethnic conflicts? If, casting a cursory glance at Table 1, one makes an attempt to succinctly characterize the population's psychological status in the sphere of interethnic relations, then the word 'guarded' seems to be most appropriate. In neither ethnic group/nationality, including the indigenous one, can we observe a maximum (100%) manifestation of tolerance: only 79% of those polled chose to accept Ukrainians as family members, and less than a half of the respondents – Russians.

An analysis of the distribution of ethnic groups/nationalities on the social distance scale according to the ethnic intolerance index (see the far right column in Table 1) leads us to conclude that there is a certain striving for East Slavic separateness in the minds of Ukrainian people: Ukrainians, Russians, Belarussians, Poles and Ukrainian expatriates (the diaspora) have an index value of less than four points on the social distance scale, which may testify if not to a pronounced tolerance then, at least, to some positive value for it.

A number of nationalities are characterized by an intolerance index of more than five 5 points, which means, specifically, that representatives of these nationalities are not accepted in people's minds as permanent residents of Ukraine. A list of nationalities which are rejected most of all (Crimean Tatars, Georgians, Arabs, Negroes, Gypsies and the Vietnamese) may lead one to surmise that the underlying reason for such rejection is an association in people's minds of these nationalities with a threat of international or interethnic conflicts. Thus, a fear of interethnic/international clashes is, in our opinion, a result of general cautiousness as a basic character trait of Ukraine's population, rather than an indication of ethnic/national intolerance. It is probably this same guardedness that on the one hand helps avoid large-scale interethnic confrontation and, on the other, facilitates the formation of a certain (as it were, 'soft') type of xenophobia, separation from all 'aliens'. That is precisely why ethnic Ukrainians abroad (Ukrainian expatriates, on whom many people in Ukraine pinned great hopes for assisting them in building up independent Ukraine's economy) occupy in the minds of people in Ukraine a more remote place than Russians or Belarussians, and have an index of more than three points, which is beyond the range of the closest (friendly, neighbourly or family) ties.

In this context (the shaping of national isolation psychology), representatives of most nationalities are accepted in people's minds only as visitors to Ukraine.

Of certain interest for an analysis of ethnic/national intolerance is the position of Jews on the scale of social distance. By virtue of historical circumstances, the problem of anti-Semitism has a special if not leading place in the range of the world's problems in the field of international/interethnic relations. Historically, this issue was one of the most important interethnic problems in Ukraine. It is rather topical even nowadays, since it is closely linked with the problems of human rights protection, migration and international co-operation.

The results of international/interethnic tolerance measurements made it possible to see that problem in a somewhat different light. If previously this had been a matter of anti-Semitism as such, with an emphasis on the negative attitude towards Jews alone, a comparison of attitudes to Jews with attitudes to other nationalities leads one to conclude that anti-Semitism is just one particular manifestation of a more general xenophobia – rejection of practically all nationalities or ethnic groups different from one's own: Jews far from occupy a leading place. Moreover, on the scale of social distance they are placed much closer in the mass consciousness of Ukraine's population than most other nationalities/ethnic groups. When considering the data on Ukraine as a whole, Jews are placed in the group of nationalities, which are 'driven out' by the mass consciousness beyond the range of close contacts (four points). This, however, mainly occurs because of the attitudes of rural and small town dwellers, for whom Jews as well as most other nationalities are rather 'alien'. In Kiev, however, the index of intolerance to Jews is less than four points (3.44 points), in other big cities (with more than 250,000 thousand inhabitants each) it is 3.67 points, while in small towns – 4.25 points and in villages – 4.56 points (all differences are significant at least at the level of 0.05, and between the extreme groups – at the level of 0.001).

This concrete example is a vivid illustration of the conclusion that people consider as 'friendly' those nationalities or ethnic groups with whom they have lived together for a long time on this territory. This frame of mind, reflecting an a priori mistrust of practically all nations/ethnic groups that have not lived for a long time on this territory, is typical of the value system of a closed traditionalist-archaic society. Widespread traditionalist-communitarian values are an essential obstacle in the course of the democratic transformation of society.

A low level of ethnic/national tolerance, manifested with regard to certain ethnic groups/nationalities, is but one manifestation of a low level of general ethnic/national tolerance. It is primarily a matter of xenophobia which became a real fact of life in Ukrainian society during the collapse of the totalitarian system, when the 'genie' of intolerance and distrust with regard to 'aliens' and other special groups or strata as well as to other ethnic groups and nationalities broke loose from the shackles of Communist ideology and all-round suppression of dissidence.

This conclusion is confirmed by the results of a factor analysis of the data. Factorization made it possible to single out three major factors which, combined, determined 82% of the variance in assessments. The first factor (its explanatory force was 66%) may be interpreted as the factor of 'East Slavic withdrawal', for only on the scales of assessments of Ukrainians, Russians and Belarussians were no high factor loads registered with respect to national intolerance. In other words, if someone shows intolerance towards a certain ethnic group/nationality, it is very probable that he/she will show intolerance towards most other nationalities or ethnic groups not considered by him or her as 'friendly people'. There is also another definition of the factor dominant in the minds of people, namely xenophobia.

The second and third factors are far weaker in their explanatory power (12.3% and 4.4% respectively) and characterize, in our (optimistic) opinion, a potentially positive element in the people's minds. The second factor may be termed the factor of 'general ethnic/national tolerance', since it includes high negative values for factor loads of those ethnic groups or nationalities which are rejected most of all by the mass consciousness. The structure of the third factor – 'orientation towards the West' – includes only those scales with high negative loads which characterize attitudes to representatives of developed Western countries. It is precisely these two factors, as yet rather weak but still present in the minds of people, that give us some hope for better prospects of the development of the system attitudes of Ukraine's population towards representatives of other ethnic groups/nationalities.

On the one hand, the population's general cautiousness and guardedness, rather vividly manifested in the rejection of nationalities and ethnic groups whose image is in some way associated in the mass consciousness with interethnic and international conflicts, work towards the preservation of a more or less durable peace in Ukraine at a time when other regions of the former Soviet Union are plagued with murderous interethnic feuds. On the other hand, such over-cautiousness is also leading to the creation and consolidation of a prospectless (from the point of view of building up an economically developed civilized nation) phenomenon of general national and ethnic intolerance, originating from a psychological isolation from practically all nationalities and ethnic groups which do not have a long historical record of living on the territory of Ukraine.

3 General Ethnic/National Intolerance

The phenomenon of xenophobia (established as a result of the correlation and factor analysis), the essence of which lies in the fact that manifestations of intolerance towards certain specific nationality or ethnic group are merely a special case of manifestation of more general ethnic/national intolerance, substantiate the expediency of using such an indicator as the general ethnic/national intolerance index. This index is a simple average of values of ethnic/national intolerance indicators. In calculating a simple average value of the index of general ethnic/national intolerance, attitudes towards ethnic Russians and Ukrainians as the major nationalities living on the territory of Ukraine, as well as attitudes towards Ukrainian expatriates, are not taken into account since they are representatives of the same nationalities as the indigenous population.

According to the data obtained, the general ethnic/national intolerance index of Ukraine's adult population in 1992 was 4.63 points on a seven points scale, where the value of 4 points is a mark dividing positive (tolerant) and negative (intolerant) attitudes to other nationalities/ethnic groups. One can see that the general national/ethnic tolerance of Ukraine's population has shifted to the negative end of the scale, for which reason it would be more exact to speak about a general national intolerance. Analysing the factors affecting the phenomenon in question, one can maintain that a factor's influence is positive, even if it only reduces the average level of general intolerance, rather than increasing tolerance.

4 Socio-Demographic Factors of General Ethnic Intolerance

Our analysis of socio-demographic factors of ethnic intolerance makes it possible to empirically verify the hypothesis that educational level, age and type of settlement substantially affect the level of ethnic tolerance: the higher the individual's educational level and the younger he/she is, the lower the level of general intolerance. Place of residence affects not only attitudes towards Jews, as was mentioned above, but also a general ethnic intolerance index (Table 2):

Table 2 *Levels of ethnic intolerance of various socio-demographic groups of Ukraine's population*

	Index of overall national intolerance (on a scale from 1-7)
Ukraine's population as a whole	4.63
AGE	
under 30 years	4.40
30-55 years	4.65
over 55 years	4.89
EDUCATION	
Incomplete secondary	4.91
Complete general secondary	4.61
Specialized secondary	4.58
Higher	4.38

TYPE OF SETTLEMENT	
Kiev	4.1
Large city	4.40
Small town	4.62
Village	4.86
REGION	
Kiev	4.1
the West	4.31
the Centre	4.87
the East	4.71
the South	4.71
the Crimea	4.63
ETHNIC GROUP	
Ukrainians	4.69
Ethnic Russians	4.52
Others	4.43

According to the 1992 data, regional peculiarities are as follows: the lowest level of general ethnic/national intolerance was registered in the western region, while the highest level was in the central region, which confirms the hypothesis that a level of national/ethnic tolerance is influenced by the experience of ethnic groups/nationalities living together and co-operating with other ethnic groups/nations. Poles, Hungarians, Romanians and other ethnic groups living in Ukraine are largely concentrated on the territory of the western region, while the central region is more homogeneous in its ethnic composition. Furthermore, joint ventures and business contacts intensified in the first years of the new, market-oriented economic policy, and were more developed in Western Ukraine. There is another explanation for the lower level of general ethnic intolerance in Western Ukraine: in our opinion, the region's population was oriented to market transformations in the economy to a greater extent, and, as will be shown below, market orientations are rather closely related to a lower level of ethnic intolerance.

Certain differences in the level of ethnic intolerance were registered between Ukrainians and ethnic Russians: in 1992 Ukrainians' general ethnic intolerance was somewhat higher (see Table 1; the difference is significant at the level of 0.05).

5 Ethnic Specifics of National Intolerance

The data obtained make it possible to specify differences between Ukrainians and ethnic Russians living in Ukraine with regard to their attitudes towards various ethnic groups/nationalities. Table 3 shows the results of the research for the following indicators:

- the left columns represent maximum tolerance of various ethnic/national groups – the percentage of representatives of the ethnic group in question who expressed their readiness to have close relations with representatives of the given nationality;
- the right columns show indicators of national/ethnic intolerance of each nationality/ethnic group (on a seven point scale):

Table 3 *Attitudes of Russians and Ukrainians towards representatives of various nationalities/ethnic groups*

Nationality	Ready to accept representatives of this nationality as related through marriage		Index of intolerance towards this nationality (on a scale from 1-7)	
	Ethnic Russians	*Ukrainians*	*Ethnic Russians*	*Ukrainians*
Ukrainians	69	84	1.66	1.47**
Russians	67	34	1.82	2.64**
Belarussians	38	25	2.62	2.92**
Ukrainian expatriates	18	25	3.75	3.39**
Poles	17	15	3.75	3.79
Jews	14	7	3.88	4.30**
Hungarians	12	8	4.11	4.32
Americans	12	11	4.15	4.37*
Germans	12	7	4.20	4.51**
French	12	8	4.22	4.54**
Romanians	10	6	4.50	4.61
Japanese	5	4	4.52	4.72*
Crimean Tatars	4	3	4.91	5.16**
Georgians	4	3	5.06	5.37**
Vietnamese	3	2	5.29	5.30
Arabs	6	2	5.29	5.51
Negroes			5.46	5.51
Gypsies	3	3	5.51	5.60

(* $p < 0.05$; ** $p < 0.01$)

Two regularities are very conspicuous in the data. Firstly, all the nationalities presented for assessment were arranged both by ethnic Russians and Ukrainians in the same order of rejection. Even the position 'Russians' was no exception for ethnic Russians.

Secondly, in practically all cases the intolerance indices of Ukrainians are higher, except in the case of their attitudes towards Ukrainians (both autochthonous and expatriates). Insignificant differences were registered in their attitudes towards Poles, Hungarians and Romanians as well as to nationalities which are rejected most of all both by ethnic Russians and Ukrainians (Vietnamese, Arabs, Negroes, Gypsies).

Naturally, of the most topical interest from the point of view of preserving and maintaining civil peace in Ukraine, are attitudes of ethnic Russians and Ukrainians towards each other. Ethnic Russians are the largest ethnic minority in Ukraine. As far as their historical, political and economic role in Ukraine's social life is concerned, they occupy one of the leading positions and the significance of their position increases dramatically in light of the prospects for solving problems in relations between Russia and Ukraine.

In 1992, attitudes of ethnic Russians towards Ukrainians were, as noted above, characterized by a striving for a homogeneous nation. Ethnic Russians rated Ukrainians on the scale of social distance even higher, albeit insignificantly, than their own ethnic group. This was in line with their support of the status of Ukraine as an independent (primarily in relation to Russia), sovereign state, which was demonstrated at the 1991 referendum. Underlying that orientation toward Ukraine's political and economic independence was a widespread (at that time) assumption about Ukraine's might and great economic potential which, so it was thought, could not be materialized because Ukraine had to support all the 'hangers-on' of the republics of the FSU, above all Russia. With respect to the attitudes of Ukrainians towards ethnic Russians, Table 3 indicates that the latter are indeed regarded by Ukrainians on the scale of social distance as being closer to themselves than all other ethnic groups/nationalities, yet further than the autochtonous nationality. The reasons that could explain this situation are well understood: a considerable Ukrainian part of the population, having experienced a period of Russification and imperial 'protection', is very bitter about a possible return to the times when the Union Centre used to make decisions for Ukraine without taking its people's interests into account. That is why suspicion with regard to Russia was carried over to ethnic Russians as a whole. As is usually the case when a question of national differences in attitudes to some social phenomenon arises, many people resort without a moment's hesitation to generalized ethnic or national categories, e.g., 'Russians', 'Ukrainians', etc..

The results of our research, conducted in spring 1992, revealed certain differences in the attitudinal system of representatives of one ethnic group towards various other ethnic groups living in different regions. To take an example, Ukrainians living in different regions of Ukraine have different attitudes towards various ethnic groups and, in particular, to ethnic Russians and Ukrainian expatriates (in the diaspora). Table 4 supplies data clearly mapping out the pattern of attitudes of ethnic Russians and Ukrainians towards each other in 1992, with due consideration of the factor of regional heterogeneity of attitudes of Ukraine's autochtonous population.

Table 4 *Peculiarities of attitudes of Ukrainians living in various regions of Ukraine towards Ukrainians and ethnic Russians*

	Index of intolerance (on a scale from 1-7)		
	towards Ukrainians	towards Russians	towards Ukrainians living abroad
Ukraine's population as a whole	1.55	2.45	3.48
Ukrainians	1.47	2.64	3.39
Ethnic Russians	1.66	1.82	3.75
Ukrainians in various regions			
The western region (Galicia)	1.08	2.71	1.81
The central region	1.13	2.53	3.53
The eastern region	1.52	2.23	3.74
The southern region	1.98	3.17	3.85
The Crimea	2.29	3.24	4.29

While the group of respondents representing the Crimea's Ukrainians was very small and can therefore not be considered to represent the Ukrainian population of the region with sufficient statistical reliability, we still provide the corresponding data since they reflect a general trend: ethnic Russians are rated on the scale of social distance as a group which is closer to Ukrainians than Ukrainian expatriates. Only Ukrainians in the western region are an exception to this – they rate Ukrainian expatriates closer to themselves than ethnic Russians. Thus, one can see that the socio-psychological attitudes of Ukrainians in the sphere of interethnic relations are rather different in various regions of Ukraine and this should be taken into account not only in further research but also in political decision-making.

6 Ethnic/National Intolerance Dynamics

Results of the second round of research undertaken in May 1994 make it possible to determine and describe certain trends in the development of the ethnic/national tolerance of Ukraine's population. In this connection the indicators of general and specific tolerance of Ukrainians and ethnic Russians towards each other are important.

The level of general national/ethnic tolerance can be considered, within the context of prospects for the development of society, as an indicator of the degree of readiness of the population's mass consciousness to open up and to co-operate with the world community on the basis of generally recognized democratic principles.

At the same time, indicators of attitudes of ethnic Russians and Ukrainians towards each other are indicators of internal socio-political processes, the development of which can consolidate or jeopardize civil peace and accord in Ukraine. Moreover, attitudes towards ethnic Russians largely reflect the population's attitudes towards relations with Russia. Within the general political context, one cannot disregard the fact that peace in Eastern Europe will be largely determined by the course of development of relationships between Ukraine and Russia. An aggravation of the problems of the Crimea and the Black Sea Fleet, which have become major objects of confrontation between Ukraine and Russia, evokes serious concern not only among the responsible politicians of the two sides but also from the world community as a whole. The population's support of various political actions, of both a compromising and confrontational nature, is at present an essential factor in political decision-making. In this connection, monitoring social moods and feelings, particularly those reflected in mutual ethnic tolerance, enables one to predict to a certain extent the population's reactions to changes in Ukrainian policy vis-à-vis Russia.

Table 5 shows the dynamics of levels of general national/ethnic tolerance with respect to changes which occurred in the mass consciousness of the population in various regions of Ukraine in the past two years of the new state's making.

Table 5 *Regional peculiarities of the general dynamics of national/ethnic intolerance*

Regions	Index of overall national intolerance (on a scale from 1-7)	
	1992	1994
Kiev	4.01	4.49
the western region	4.31	4.33
the central region	4.87	4.25**
the eastern region	4.71	4.64
the southern region	4.71	4.68
the Crimea	4.63	4.13*
Ukraine	4.63	4.44**

* $p < 0.05$; ** $p. < 0.01$

First of all, it should be noted that a certain drop occurred in the average level of general national/ethnic intolerance of the population of Ukraine as a whole. On the one hand, the level remains shifted to the negative side of the tolerance scale (whereby, as has been mentioned, the mark of four points divides the positive and negative sides of the scale). On the other hand, however, there is a statistically significant movement toward a greater general national/ethnic tolerance which testifies to a positive if slow trend in the evolution of the mass consciousness.

Important changes in the level of general national/ethnic tolerance took place in the minds of people in Central Ukraine. The higher level of general national tolerance in this region shows that this formerly politically indifferent area with prevailing traditionalist-archaic orientations (where local interests supercede all other) is beginning to become rather actively involved in the political life of the country and, in some cases, to substantially influence the course of political developments. For example, the changes in the mass consciousness of the region's population found their reflection in the outcomes of the 1994 presidential elections. In the past, Central Ukraine had been fairly homogeneous in its political orientations (an assertion confirmed both by various data of public opinion polls and referendum results), thus enabling the integration of a number of *oblasts* into a single region. However, the outcomes of the 1994 presidential elections allow one to conclude that the population became differentiated in this region, where the choice between Leonid Kravchuk (the ex-president) and Leonid Kuchma (the encumbent president) divided the population, as the voting confirmed, into Left Bank and Right Bank central subregions (with certain western Ukrainian and eastern Ukrainian orientations).

A rise of the national intolerance index in Kiev is not statistically significant due to the small number of those polled (90 people) and the variability in individual assessments.

As far as the dynamics of tolerance of Ukraine's population towards various nationalities are concerned (Table 6), one can see that changes in opposite directions took place. Set against a background of a rather stable level of intolerance towards representatives of developed Western countries (Americans and Germans – here the changes are statistically insignificant), the general trends seems to be that intolerance towards ethnic groups living in Ukraine (Crimean Tatars, gypsies, Jews) decreased, while it rose with respect to Eastern European neighbours (Poles and Hungarians).

Table 6 *Dynamics of tolerance of Ukraine's population towards various nationalities*

Nationalities	Index of national intolerance (on a scale from 1-7)		
	April 1992 N = 1752	*May 1994* *N = 1807*	Change in index
Ukrainians	1.55	1.83	+0.28**
Russians	2.45	2.25	-0.20**
Belarussians	2.85	2.70	-0.15*
Jews	4.18	3.82	-0.36**
Americans	4.31	4.42	+0.11
Poles	3.77	4.45	+0.68**
Germans	4.43	4.48	+0.05
Crimean Tatars	5.09	4.55	-0.54**
Slovaks	-	4.55	
Hungarians	4.24	4.59	+0.35**
Moldavians	-	4.59	
Romanians	4.56	4.69	+0.13*
Serbians	-	4.77	
Georgians	5.26	4.86	-0.40**
Turks	-	4.91	
Gypsies	5.55	5.09	-0.46**

(* $p < 0.05$; ** p.< 0.01)

The rise in tolerance towards Georgians can be primarily explained by the fact that certain political forces in Ukraine actively supported the Georgian side in the

Georgian-Abkhazian conflict (more specifically, many Ukraine's citizens went on relief missions to Georgia in 1993-1994). Due to a rather wide pro-Georgian propaganda campaign on the Ukrainian TV Channel UTAR and the involvement of a part of Ukraine's population in the events in Georgia (family and friendly ties and contacts with people who supported the Georgian side), an increase in tolerance of Georgians occured.

7 Dynamics of Relationships between Ukrainians and Ethnic Russians

A rising national tolerance towards ethnic Russians and a declining tolerance towards Ukrainians are main trends in the development of relationships between Ukrainians and ethnic Russians (see Table 6).

Table 7 gives the data characterizing regional peculiarities of dynamics of attitudes towards Ukrainians and ethnic Russians .

Table 7 *Dynamics of the Population's Attitudes to Ukrainians and Ethnic Russians: Regional Peculiarities*

	Index of intolerance to Ukrainians		Index of intolerance to Russians	
Regions	1992	1994	1992	1994
Kiev	1.67	1.65	2.17	2.08
the western region	1.37	1.75**	3.14	2.97
the central region	1.33	1.41	2.58	1.79**
the eastern region	1.58	2.03**	2.05	2.24*
the southern region	1.86	2.02	2.84	2.22**
the Crimea	2.27	2.76	1.83	2.34*
Ukraine	1.55	1.83**	2.45	2.25**

* $p < 0.05$; ** $p < 0.01$

Tolerance of Ukrainians significantly decreased in the eastern and western (!) regions of Ukraine – regions most sensitive to interethnic relations between ethnic Russians and Ukrainians. The same trend is characteristic of the southern region but because of a scattering of individual assessments these changes are statistically insignificant. These changes are, in our opinion, a reflection of a disillusionment with the idea of national revival by way of isolationism and a greater orientation towards partnership with Russia.

The most significant rise in tolerance of ethnic Russians occurred in the central and southern regions of Ukraine. The Crimea and the southern region showed a drop in tolerance both of Ukrainians and ethnic Russians, which reflects the aggravation of the problem of Russian-Ukrainian relations precisely in this region. Linguistic policy (specifically, demands to institute Russian as the second official language in the country) may be a factor which contributed to the aggravation of the problem.

Ukraine has a specific linguistic situation: there are important regional differences in the number of people using this or that language in everyday communication. Table 8 shows the data illustrating regional differences in the use of languages in everyday communication. Answers to the question „What language do you use for communication in your family?" were regarded as indicators of a preferred language use.

Table 8 *Regional peculiarities of preferred language use in family communication (May 1994; in percentage for each region)*

Regions	„What language do you use for communication in your family?"		
	Only Ukrainian	Only Russian	Both, depending on circumstances
Kiev	15	39	46
The western region	79	5	16
The central region	60	8	32
The eastern region	13	53	35
The southern region	22	47	31
The Crimea	4	86	11
Ukraine	37	33	30

If on average in Ukraine the proportions of people who prefer to speak only Ukrainian or only Russian, as well as those who use both languages, are approximately the same, in each individual region one of the two languages is prevalent in family communication. In Kiev, almost half of its inhabitants use both languages. The central and especially western regions are mainly Ukrainian-speaking, while in the Crimea and in the eastern and southern regions Russian is obviously dominant. Therefore, a hard-line state language policy which stipulates that all official documents should be written in Ukrainian only cannot but evoke inner tension, especially in people who have a poor command of the only official language. Many people in these regions voted for Leonid Kuchma at the 1994 presidential election largely because his election programme contained a promise to grant Russian the status of the second official language. Incidentally, orientation to strengthening economic ties with Russia was another important point in the programme of the would-be president.

The greater orientation of Ukraine's population towards economic ties with Russia was brought about by improvements in Russia (as compared with Ukraine) in the two most important components of people's living standards: higher average wages and a stronger currency unit (the purchasing power of the Russian rouble is higher in Ukraine than that of the Ukrainian coupon). It is precisely this factor which in our opinion played a decisive part in the electoral behaviour of the Central Left Bank subregion of Ukraine in the 1994 presidential elections. Under the present economic conditions in Ukraine, when wages cannot provide for a subsistence level, three-quarters of Ukraine's population (according to data of the sociological poll, conducted with the author's participation in February 1991 by the sociological service of the *Democratic Intiatives Centre*), survive solely on products grown on personal plots of land attached to their houses (50% constantly, 25% periodically). Many people in the central region, especially in Left Bank Ukraine, prefer to sell products from their personal plots in Russia, because, as it has been noted, the purchasing power of the Russian rouble in Ukraine is higher than that of the Ukrainian coupon.

Thus, the major reason for the rise in national tolerance of ethnic Russians lies, in our opinion, in the better economic situation in Russia as compared with Ukraine.

The data obtained also made it possible to establish a significant link between the socio-economic attitudes of people and their level of general national/ethnic tolerance.

8 Influence of Socio-Economic Orientations of Population on National/Ethnic Tolerance

Put in its most general form, the interconnection between socio-economic orientations and national tolerance is characterized by the following regularity: the more people are oriented towards market reforms in the economy, the higher their national/ethnic tolerance level tends to be. As an example we can provide data that illustrate the interdependence between general attitude to economic reforms and general national/ethnic tolerance index: those people who advocate a complete transition to a market economy have a lower index of general national/ethnic intolerance than those who would like to return to the socialist economy of the Brezhnev era of stagnation (see Table 9).

Table 9 *Influence of Socio-Economic Orientations on National/Ethnic Tolerance*

„What is your attitude to economic transformations in Ukraine?"	Index of overall national intolerance (on a scale from 1-7)
There must be a complete transition to the market economy	4.15
There must be only some individual reforms	4.62
The country's economy should be brought back to the state it was *in at the* beginning of the perestroika	4.61

A similar trend has been revealed in the analysis of the interdependence between national tolerance and other indicators of socio-economic orientations. For example, national/ethnic tolerance is lower among those people who prefer 'low prices and the accompanying shortage of products and goods' than in those who prefer 'high prices and the accompanying sufficient supply of goods and food products'. National/ethnic tolerance is lower in those people who have negative attitudes towards business, entrepreneurship, private property, etc.

On the basis of these data one can suggest that as a result of radical economic reforms aimed at establishing private property and an improvement of Ukraine's economic situation, the national/ethnic tolerance of its population will increase. The worsening of the economic situation may lead to a lower self-tolerance of Ukraine's population as just one form of self-respect and confidence in its own strength and the feasibility of building its new state.

9 Main Conclusions

1. The values of indicators of national/ethnic tolerance of Ukraine's adult population towards various nationalities and ethnic groups testify to the fact that in the first stage of making a new independent nation, a striving for national and state isolationism was an essential element of the mass consciousness. The urge for separateness manifested itself in the fact that the population's attitude was most tolerant mainly towards those ethnic groups/nationalities which, historically, lived on the territory of Ukraine. Most nationalities/ethnic groups are shifted by the mass consciousness along the scale of social distance beyond the mark of close contacts. The greatest suspiciousness and guardedness is displayed with respect to those nationalities/ethnic groups whose image is somehow associated, to a greater or lesser extent, with interethnic or international conflicts.

2. Manifestations of intolerance (non-acceptance) towards some specific nationality or ethnic group are a special case of manifestation of a more general national xenophobia (distrust and suspiciousness with respect to all 'aliens'). Therefore, if someone is intolerant of one nationality or ethnic group, he/she is very likely to be intolerant to all other nationalities or ethnic groups which he/she does not consider as 'friendly'.
3. The level of general national/ethnic tolerance increased somewhat in the first two years (1992-1994) of Ukraine's independence and this may be an indication of positive, albeit slow trends in changes of mass consciousness on the way to an open democratic society.

   The most noticeable dynamics of general national/ethnic tolerance were registered in the central region of Ukraine, which reflects overall changes in the minds of people in this region. These changes are in line with the increase of this region's role in the general political situation in Ukraine.
4. In 1992-1994, important changes occurred in the system of relationships between Ukrainians and ethnic Russians: the population's tolerance towards Ukrainians went down (even in the western region), while it went up with respect to ethnic Russians. In our opinion, this can be explained by the disillusionment of Ukraine's population with the idea of national revival by way of isolationism (brought about by the lowering of living standards and quality of life) as well as by the strengthening of orientations towards economic ties and co-operation with Russia.

   Russia's advantages in the economic sphere (as compared with Ukraine) are a major factor of changes in the system of relationships between Ukrainians and ethnic Russians. The pace of economic reforms in Russia is higher than in Ukraine and hence a) the higher level of average wages in Russia b) the higher purchasing power of the Russian rouble on the territory of Ukraine.

   The following are, in our opinion, the main factors which can lead to a higher level of national/ethnic tolerance among Ukraine's population:
   a) real economic reforms (above all, a definitive legislative support of private property accompanied by social protection and maintenance of the disabled and senior citizens) and, in this connection, greater socio-economic orientations of the population towards the market economy, which are in turn closely connected with greater democratic orientations towards an open society;

b) a flexible linguistic policy in the field of official language, taking into account regional peculiarities related to predominantly used languages of communication.

The decline in living standards and quality of life are key factors which may negatively influence not only general national/ethnic tolerance but also tolerance of Ukrainians (including Ukrainians' self-tolerance). A further decline in living standards (especially to the limit when even the highest official salary or wages are considerably less than the subsistence level) will inevitably lead not only to a lower confidence in power structures but also to disbelief in one's own strength and capabilities. In such a situation a reverse movement of the people towards socialist 'values': 'anti-market' orientations, 'witchhunts for enemies of the people' (who are allegedly responsible for low living standards), an increase in suspicion with respect to all 'aliens', and therefore intolerance.

8

Ethnic Areas in Modern Russia:
A Comparative Analysis of Ethno-Political Risk

Vladimir Kolossov and Andrei Treivish

Methods of Research

What is a national minority? It is one of the native peoples, living in a given territory (if so, one may ask whether Hungarians or Russians, who have been living in Tatarstan since the end of the 16th century are native or not)? Or is it any national group of people that is less numerous than the nation that represents a 'majority' on that territory? Obviously, a 'national minority' is a broad notion, covering a continuum from immigrants, who have arrived for permanent residence and are scattered all over a given territory, up to native ethnic groups that predominate in certain areas of compact residence. This continuum includes a great variety of intermediates:

- diasporas (self-reproducing groups of another culture, that have been living for centuries in one country and are deeply integrated into its social fibre[1]);
- peoples who are separated from each other by state borders or who do not have a historical motherland;
- various other intermediate cases that were typical for the former USSR, i.e., cases where national minorities live compactly in one place but are scattered in another, etc.

In this study we consider only those minorities who live in 'their' ethnic areas. The notion of an ethnic area or a national minority region corresponds, in our opinion, to at least the following two criteria:

---

1 See, for instance, the special issue devoted to this topic in *Espace Géographique* 1994, no. 3; and especially Kolossov V., T. Galkina and M. Kouibychev. "La géographie des diasporas: une approche théorique et l'exemple des communautés Arménienne, Grecque et Juive dans l'ex-URSS." *Espace géographique* 1994, no. 3.

1. the minority has within a certain state its *own ethnic territory*, where it lives compactly; and
2. the minority's *population exceeds a certain threshold value*.

Without its own national territory a national minority is not entitled to any form of territorial autonomy, nor can any regional, separatist or irredentist movements be formed; even the formation of cultural organisations is stunted. For example, in Ukraine, Russians mostly live in big cities and do not have their own ethnic areas. Their situation is therefore very different from that of Russians living in Eastern Ukraine or on the Crimea.

It is evident that the bigger a minority is, the more chances it has (all other things being equal) to press for its rights, to struggle for a higher political status and, lastly, to attract the attention of the international community. It is also clear that there were so many minorities in the former Soviet Union (ethnologists still differ as to their exact number, but most probably there were over 100) that it is hardly possible to take stock of all their areas. Moreover, in most of these areas national minorities comprise quite a small proportion of the overall population. The criteria for a 'noticeable' minority also depend on the dimension of countries. In Europe, for instance, they are smaller than in Russia: many western European reference books and monographs estimate this threshold as 30-50,000 people. For Russia the threshold should probably be raised to 100,000 except for the sparsely populated Far North, where small native nations play an important role in keeping the ethnic balance.

Nevertheless, these criteria do not seem sufficient. Take, for instance, the German Poles, who are concentrated in the Ruhr. Yet one can hardly regard the Ruhr as the ethnic area of the Polish national minority, for it is obvious that the German Poles will never be able to claim territorial autonomy. The Russian minority in Tallinn, even though constituting almost half of the population of Estonia in 1989, does not make up an ethnic area, whereas Russians in north-eastern Estonia, adjacent to Russia, do undoubtedly form such an area. Therefore, the third criterion of an ethnic area is the availability or probability of *claims to any kind of national or territorial autonomy*, or the emergence of separatist and irredentist movements.

To compare different ethnic areas in Russia, one must first of all select a number of variables that can be quantitatively arranged to characterise diverse aspects of the 'nationalities problem'. Secondly, since a) national minorities differ sharply as to their population numbers and other indicators, b) the quantitative parameters have to be compared with the qualitative ones and, c) because in some cases the required data is not available or difficult to find; one should express these variables in interval points. Selected indicators are directly connected with the intensity of the national dilemma: the higher this or that indicator is, the more tense the situation is, or vice versa. However, the difficulty here is that many interdependencies are far from being straightforward, hence, it is not easy to make up a linear scale. Some interesting approaches to this problem can be found in literature[2], but they refer only to limited territories – West European countries, as a rule. Moreover, these studies make use of a comparatively small number of indicators (5-7 as a rule) some of which, like net migration rate, are rather dubious.

For example, how does the level of living standards of a compact national minority relate to its own appraisal of its situation? Experience of foreign countries, as well as that of the republics of the former USSR shows that low living standards (income, etc.) in the ethnic regions relative to the national average figures, causes sharp criticism of federal policy. At the same time, 'rich' national regions are also dissatisfied with their position, believing that the central government is funding the others at their expense. Likewise, it is undesirable when the population of an ethnic area 'vote with their feet' (i.e., leave the area): a negative net migration rate is evidence of social hardships. Equally negative, however, is when the ethnic area turns into a strong attraction pole for immigrants: their inflow tends to change the ethnic balance and to contribute to social tension.

It is clear a priori that inter-ethnic relations are too complicated to be measured by a strictly formalised system of indicators. Ideological and informational factors, as well as the behaviour of elites and decision-makers also play an important role. Therefore, estimates of inter-ethnic tension can only be partially formal. Accuracy is ensured in this case by defining a range of co-ordinated parameters and by establishing an expert system of evaluation of these parameters (i.e., the system based upon a 'point-scale', or 'grade-scale').

We have tried to select the 16 most relevant parameters that more or less meet all the above-mentioned requirements. The values of these parameters have been divided into 3-4 groups: from 0 to 3 (4) points – the more points an ethnic area 'scores' on a given parameter, the greater is its 'contribution' to the overall political tension. So, by adding up the points from all groups of parameters and summing

---

2 Anderson, A.B. „Ethnic Nationalism and Regional Autonomy in Canada and Western Europe." In Pramdas, R.R., S.V. Samarasinghe and A.B. Anderson (eds.). *Secessionist Movements in Comparative Perspective*. London: Pinter, 1990; Krejci, J. and V. Velimsky. *Ethnic and Political Nations in Europe*. London: Croom Helm, 1981; and *Qualitative and Quantitative Strategies*. Berkeley, Los Angeles, London: University of California Press, 1989.

them, we can to some extent 'measure' the intensity of the nationalities problem, or the factors leading to its aggravation.

The first three parameters describe the *potential influence* of a national minority in its own area and in the country as a whole: its absolute number, its 'share' in the population of the area and of the whole country. The second group of parameters characterises the *geopolitical position* of the ethnic area. We proceeded from the notion that if an ethnic area is isolated or located deep inside the territory of the state, this will not be conducive to forces that initiate nationalities conflicts. Quite the opposite happens when representatives of a given national minority that has its own area can rely (at least potentially) on the support of fellow-countrymen in another area, or on the assistance of a friendly ethnic group in an adjacent area. Lastly, the greatest potential risk of conflicts arises when the ethnic area borders on the territory of a state where the same nationality is predominant.

Geopolitically, the distribution of a national minority within its area defines the latter's boundaries: if a minority is scattered or mixed up with the state's titular nationality, then it acquires a number of peculiarities likening it to a diaspora, which has found a stable social niche (certainly, there are examples to the contrary, although they are not numerous). On the other hand, clear-cut boundaries of the ethnic area, coupled with regional segregation, contribute considerably to the minority's alienation from the rest of the state.

The third group of parameters describes the group's *cultural and linguistic situation*: the proportion of the minority which still speaks its ethnic mother tongue, the status of this language in the state or in the ethnic area and whether this area practically coincides with the boundaries of the national and territorial autonomies.

The fourth group of parameters concerns the *amount of time elapsed* since the minorities emerged, since their statehood and the boundaries of their national and territorial formations were established. A minority's general state depends on the peripeteia of its modern history: the 'younger' a minority is, the more likely it is to experience feelings of 'historical resentment', to harbour aspirations of revenge and that it will seek to change its destiny (the most vivid examples being Serbs in the former Yugoslavia and Russians in some of the FSU regions).

On the other hand, time, as a rule, tends to reconcile a minority with its position. As years go by, concessions are made with respect to its (minority) status and cultural rights (certainly, there are exceptions – the 'non-linear' changes of the ethno-political situation in time: suffice it to remember the Kurds and Northern Ireland). First and foremost, we have chosen for analysis those ethnic areas that were integrated into one and the same state well *before 1918* and where the national minorities are quite 'old'. This data itself corresponds to the first large-scale alteration of the map of Europe, completed immediately after World War I. In *1944*, fourteen peoples were deported. In the wake of World War II and the subsequent geopolitical changes in Europe which legalised the pre-war and post-war territorial acquisitions of the USSR, a number of ethnic areas have either disappeared altogether (such as in the case of the Volga Germans and the Crimean Tatars), or changed their state affiliation. These cases represent the second group of 'younger' minorities. Eventually, the third fundamental geopolitical transformation started in *1989* as a result of the collapse of socialist regimes in Eastern European countries and later – the disintegration of Yugoslavia, the USSR and Czechoslovakia. This transformation is not yet complete, but it has already resulted in profound and irrevocable changes in the status of many ethnic areas. Some ethnic groups have restored their own statehood or have gained it for the first time; others found themselves split up by new state borders which resulted in the formation of new minorities, whom we have included in the third group. On this parameter, this group has the highest conflict potential.

The events of 1989-1994 have shown that gaining statehood for even for a short period of time, i.e., just a few years or even months as is the case with some nations, is of great importance for the current ethno-political situation. After acquiring sovereignty and independence, the Baltic states and Georgia have reasserted the constitutional norms that were first adopted at the time of their original independence. The Ukrainian nationalist movement recalls the practice of the ethereal republic that existed for a few months in 1918. The Tatar movement *Ittifaq* [Freedom] – a radical wing of the Tatar Public Centre – invariably looks back to the long-gone events of 1552, when the Kazan Khanate was annexed to Moscovy. Therefore, the experience of having had or not had statehood is one of the most important characteristics of the political history of a given national minority.

Furthermore, the less the boundaries of the titular minority autonomy have changed, the less grounds nationalist forces have to demand alteration of the political map. As the study of the American geographer A. Murphy shows[3], so-called historical arguments are often used in territorial disputes and claims, although this argumentation often does not prove anything. Our own work[4] have illustrated the

---

3 Murphy, 1992.

4 Glezer, O.B., V.A. Kolossov, N.V. Petrov, L.V. Smirnyagin and A.I. Treivish. *Rossiiskaya Gazeta* 28 March 1991(special issue); Glezer, O.B., V.A. Kolossov, N.V. Petrov, L.V.

popularity of 'historical' arguments in ethno-territorial conflicts in the former USSR: they account for a high percentage of national territorial claims or claims to change the status of ethnic groups.

National self-consciousness is rooted in multifarious sources. Most vividly it is manifested in the use of the ethnic group's 'titular' language (the mother tongue may also well be a 'borrowed' one). The following simple gradation here is obvious:

- the absolute majority of the ethnic group speaks its mother tongue within its area (the conflict potential is the highest);
- the national language is still alive, but is spoken only partly within the minority;
- the minority has practically lost its original mother tongue (the probability of ethno-political tension is the lowest).

Religion is also a basis for national self-identification. If a minority belongs to the same confession as the titular nationality, or (in more complicated cases) to one of the major confessions, the likelihood of conflicts is lower. In the opposite case, religious contradictions may be extremely acute which is typical not only for Russia and the FSU, but for the whole of the 'contact zone' between the Orthodox and Islamic worlds (Cyprus, the Balkans, the Caucasus).

The *economic basis* of the ethno-political situation is affected by the ethnic area's relative position of vis-à-vis other regions. It is a bad sign when the area is poor and its internal gross product (IGP) per capita is much lower than the state's average – the ethnic group may then feel deprived of the country's wealth (as is the case with Chechnya). However, a similarly negative effect is produced when the ethnic area's industry is more advanced than that in other parts of the country – then the minority may develop a suspicion that central authorities take away a good part of its product and redistribute it among other regions where 'lazy' titular nationalities lives. The minority may also believe that central authorities are artificially lowering its living standard and thwarting its social development (Flanders in Belgium, Slovenia in former Yugoslavia, the Baltic republics in the former USSR). That is why we have labelled the situation where the IGP per capita in the ethnic area approximates the state's average as a 'zero' level of conflict potential on this parameter, and as a maximum level – the situation when the IGP deviates greatly from the average.

Smirnyagin and A.I. Treivish "Subekty federatsy: kakimi im byt? [Subjects of the Federation: Which Ones?]" *Polis* 1991, no. 4: 149-159; and Kolossov V., O. Glezer and N. Petrov. "Ethnoterritorial conflicts in the former USSR." *International Boundaries Research Unit Briefing* (Durham, UK, IBRU) 1992, no. 2.

Moreover, we have assessed each ethnic area's position on the 'centre – half-periphery – periphery' scale. Omitting well-known aspects of this concept, which were given full coverage in a special work[5], we would like to underline that these notions include a great many long-term structural parameters such as a branch-type industry structure, the character of inter-regional and international economic relations etc. A chart from the above-mentioned book was used in order to parametrize this indicator.

Finally, the sixth group of parameters describes the *level of political mobilisation* within the ethnic minority area, that is the ethnic parties (similar to the Tatar Public Centre and *Ittifaq*) which became significant due to the results of the parliamentary or local elections; 'non-institutional' forms of political mobilisation, often even more dangerous, such as instances of violence and terror (0 or 1 point on the scale of assessment of the ethno-political situation), illegal armed formations, military actions or civil war (these were assessed at 3 points, taking into consideration their extreme danger for the ethnic region).

Expert evaluations obtained by the authors, the authors' own experience in the study of ethnic and regional conflicts and elections in the former USSR were used for estimating the parameters of this group of indicators[6], as well as monitoring of major Russian periodicals collected by the Centre of Geopolitical Studies of the Institute of the Russian Academy of Sciences.

The experience of the USSR and Yugoslavia, as well as some other federative states that were totally or partially founded on national principles (Czechoslovakia, India, Nigeria, Belgium), underscores the role played by national and territorial formations in the creation of national political elites, intelligentsia, entrepreneurs,

---

5 Gritsai, O.V., G.V. Ioffe and A.I. Treivish. *Tsentr i periferiya v regionalnom razvity* [The Centre and the Periphery in Regional Development]. Moscow: Nauka, 1991.

6 Glezer, O.B., V.A. Kolossov, N.V. Petrov, L.V. Smirnyagin and A.I. Treivish. *Rossiiskaya Gazeta* 28 March 1991(special issue); Glezer, O.B., V.A. Kolossov, N.V. Petrov, L.V. Smirnyagin and A.I. Treivish "Subekty federatsy: kakimi im byt? [Subjects of the Federation: Which Ones?]" *Polis* 1991, no. 4: 149-159; and Kolossov V., O. Glezer and N. Petrov. "Ethnoterritorial conflicts in the former USSR." *International Boundaries Research Unit Briefing* (Durham, UK, IBRU) 1992, no. 2; Kolossov, V.A., N.V. Petrov and L.V. Smirnyagin (eds.). *Vesna-89* [Spring-89], Moscow, 1990; Kolossov, V. "Electoral geography of the former USSR: retrospective analysis and some theoretical conclusions." In *The New Political Geography of Eastern Europe*. O'Loughlin, J. and H. van der Wusten (eds.). London: Belhaven, 1993: 189-213; Kolossov, V.A. "Narod ne bezmolstvuet, no vprok li urok? [The People Do Not Keep Silent. But Is the Lesson Learnt?]" *Rossiiskaya federatsiya* 1994, no. 3: 13-15; Zubov, A.B. and V.A. Kolossov "Chto ishchet Rossiya (tsennostnye orientatsii rossiiskikh izbiratelei) [What Is Russia Looking For? (Value Orientations of Russian Voters)]." *Polis* (Political Studies) 1994, no. 1: 93-112.

among whom specific interests arise. These groups may attempt to realise their interests, to play the 'nationalities game' by making use of their special status as autonomies, even when the titular population constitutes a small minority. All this is still vividly exemplified by the conduct of 'old' elites in many Russian republics. For instance, 'oil generals' from the northern autonomous regions have not relinquished their hopes of using their territories' special status in order to separate them from their respective *oblasts* and to allow them to establish links with external markets. Therefore, the status of being a national or territorial autonomy or not (both in the past and at present) is so important for a given ethnic area with respect to its political potential.

The results of our calculations and assessments are presented in tables 1 and 2. This analysis poses several major questions which we will try to answer further in our discussion:

- How do national minorities and ethnic areas correlate, where and why do they coincide – even if classical diasporas (such as Jewish, Armenian, Greek and others) are not considered? Why and where is the number of areas less than the number of minorities, and what is the result of this?
- Which republic and what part of Russia is more multinational, if judged by the number of ethnic areas and minorities living there? In which of the newly formed independent states and in the whole of Russia is the ethnic and political situation the most tense?
- What is the contribution of each block of variables to the general variation of the total, or, put more simply, why is the situation in one ethnic area more tense than in the other?
- Finally, what is the situation in the CIS and in Russia like compared to the situation in Western and Central Europe? What conclusions can be made from these comparisons?

2 Ethnic Areas and Minorities

The number of ethnic (sub-ethnic) areas singled out according to our research methods is usually a little lower than the number of national minorities as we have defined them (having not less then 50 thousand people, except for the peoples of the North and the title nations of 'autonomies'). This is due to the scattering of numerous peoples of the former USSR all over its large territory (plus their mobility and predominantly urban concentration). For example – Gypsies, who have no ethnic area of their own, Jews, Armenians, to a certain extent Greeks, Tatars (outside of Russia), and even Russians, in some of the new states. The unique case is Armenia, where not a single ethnic area has been singled out, although according to the census of 1989 there were three small minorities, Azerbaidzhanis being the largest of these, which due to well-known reasons have practically disappeared.

On the other hand, one and the same minority in a large country may form several separate, comparatively compact areas. For instance, Tatars and Ukrainians in Russia have three ethnic areas each; Russians in Ukraine have two and in Kazakhstan there are four areas (large ones – in the North and South, plus two island-like industrial areas). This brings the number of ethnic areas closer to the number of minorities in the overall population and sometimes even leads to the predominance of the former.

Table 1 shows that the total number of ethnic groups in their areas is notably lower than the overall number of the minority population – all in all 48.5 million people against 71.1 million –, although in Ukraine these figures almost coincide because the East-Ukrainian and Crimean areas cover the main part of the numerous Russian minority. Furthermore, we have singled out two specific areas of sub-ethnic and religious minorities: the so-called Pripyat *polishchuks* [inhabitants of Polesye – 'the forested region' – in Ukraine and Belarus – translator's note] and Western Ukrainian Uniates [members of the Uniate Church – translator's note], data about whom is not available from the census (without them, the total inhabitants of ethnic areas in Ukraine still number eight million people, belonging to national minorities, which comes close to the average proportion). These latter minorities are also represented in Belarus, although their number is smaller there. The most important point to be stressed, however, is that there are no grounds for marking out a Russian ethnic area in Belarus – Russians live all over the republic, at least in all of its big cities, without the slightest alienation from the 'titular' and other peoples. For this reason, the number of nationals in ethnic areas of Belarus is considerably lower than the overall population of minorities. The Polish ethnic area is the largest one in Belarus according to the above criteria. Due to similar reasons it is impossible to single out Belarussian ethnic areas in Russia.

The main 'territorially delineated' minority in six FSU countries out of 15 does not coincide with the main one in terms of 'gross population'. In Russia, the index of the total population in ethnic areas unexpectedly puts the Cossacks in first place, a sub-ethnic group, which ethnically is rather heterogeneous in various regions (including the four areas we have singled out). However, at the level of separate ethnic areas it is that of the Tatars which stands out most starkly (in Tatarstan proper and in the adjacent territories of the neighbouring subjects of the Russian Federation there live about 2.3 million people) which corresponds to the fact that the Tatars are the largest ethnic minority in Russia. In Turkmenistan and Kirgizstan compact areas of Uzbeks lead according to these parameters, while the numerically main minority, Russians, is extensively scattered.

All of the above-mentioned points underline the originality of our study which differs from the traditional exploration of ethnic minorities. Strictly speaking, minorities in their ethnic areas possess all the characteristics of minorities in general and suffer from the typical problems. Moreover, they generate specific problems for respective countries connected more or less with their aspirations of territorial autonomy and self-determination.

The most influential ethnic areas in terms of 'non-titular' nationalities are in Ukraine: the average national minority, having its own area in this country, counts 1,368,000 people, which is three times greater than in Russia. Even the absolute population of 'area-type' national minorities in Ukraine is not much lower than in Russia (13.7 million and 15.8 million respectively). So, under equal conditions, the national minorities in Russia – smaller and more scattered – are less 'dangerous' for the territorial integrity and unity of the country. In a certain sense, Ukraine is a more multinational state than Russia.

It is significant that no matter how extensively the numerous Russian communities are scattered throughout the largest Ukrainian cities, there are still two large Russian ethnic areas – in the East of Ukraine and in the Crimea. In both areas Russians dominate, if one takes into account the influence of the Russian language and the dual national consciousness of many ethnic Ukrainians, who themselves feel partly Russian and partly Ukrainian at the same time[7]. As for Ukrainians in Russia, one must note that despite their large overall population in this country (4.3 million people according to the 1989 census), their proportion in the population of the three main Ukrainian areas (the south-east of European Russia, Ussuriisk-Amur and Tyumen' regions) does not exceed a few percent and only in the Tyumen' *oblast'* did the majority of Ukrainians declare their mother tongue to be their native language (these Ukrainians represent the 'new wave' of immigration, linked with exploration of oil and gas resources). Scattered throughout Russian cities and

7 Tishkov, V.A. "Strategiya i mekhanizmy natsionalnoy politiki v Rossiiskoi Federatsii [Strategy and mechanisms of the national policy in the Russian Federation]." *Etnograficheskoe Obozrenie* 1993, no. 5: 12-34.

villages, the Ukrainians have for a long time gone without their national schools, societies, press, etc., and have to some extent lost their national identity[8]. The most vivid example, however, is the practical disappearance – through ‘creeping’ Russification – of a large Ukrainian area in Kuban, which did exist back in the 1930s (its ‘remnants’ can be traced in Kushchev region and the nearby north-western region of Krasnodar krai, where the descendants of the Ukrainian Cossacks live).

Ukraine and Kazakhstan – the second largest states after Russia – have the greatest number of ethnic areas – ten each. It is therefore not surprising that Kazakhstan – a former ‘laboratory of socialist internationalism’ where 21% of marriages were multinational, occupies second place after Ukraine in the average population of minorities in their areas and the third place after Russia and Ukraine – in their absolute population. There are also large ethnic areas in Uzbekistan. In other Central Asian republics the number of people in ethnic areas, though smaller than the FSU average, is nevertheless fairly substantial if compared with the overall population. This is not so in the Transcaucasus, where of all newly independent states only Armenia has become an almost mono-national state after the deportation of Azerbaidzhani population in 1989-1990 (but the price Armenians have already paid and will still have to pay is enormous, if one takes into account that in 1993 Armenia alone lost 300,000 inhabitants who emigrated to the countries of the ‘near’ and ‘far abroad’.

3 Significance of Ethnic and Political Tension Factors

It is easy to see that the values of some variables such as ‘non-institutionalised’ political mobilisation of the population, or the overall population figures have been intentionally exaggerated by the authors in order to stress their role (the scale in these cases has 4 points (grades) instead of 3 or 2). Nevertheless, the application of our methods to the concrete situation has underscored the significance of two groups of parameters, namely the economic situation and cultural and historical identity of a national minority (prevalence and the status of the titular language, religious discrepancies, experience of having statehood). These two groups of parameters reflect about 41 % of the final, ‘synthetic’ index of tension. Cultural factors have, however, the most significant impact on the situation in the Baltic states, in Turkmenistan, Kirgizstan and Kazakhstan. In Moldova, the conflict with

8 For a more detailed analysis of this phenomenon see the recent discussion in *Nezavisimaya Gazeta* 29 April 1994.

Transdnestria has not had an exclusively ethnic character and thus the national identity factor here is minimal.

The unfavourable economic situation exerted the greatest influence on ethnic areas in Russia and Belarus, many of which are located in the peripheral, backward parts of these countries. The most typical example is that of the North Caucasian republics which by many social indicators such as the correlation between inflation and people's income (at least according to the official statistics); infant mortality rate; number of kindergartens; hospitals, etc. invariably occupy the lowest positions in the Russian Federation[9]. Some Siberian autonomies, Amur and the northern ethnic areas are in a similarly difficult situation.

Ethnic areas in Russia are much less influenced by recent historical developments than those in other republics. Russian territories that are populated by minorities seldom change their state status (except for Tuva), and minorities remain as such under different political regimes and state frontiers. 'Historical' variables seem to be more important for Ukraine, Azerbaidzhan and Tadzhikistan than for other CIS states.

The average estimate of political mobilisation in all 53 ethnic areas of Russia is not particularly high, but it makes its tangible 'contribution' to the general index of ethno-political tension, along with Moldova and Azerbaidzhan, where absolute values of these variables are rather high.

4 Ethno-Political Tension in the New States and in Their Ethnic Areas

One can compare ethno-political tension in different parts of the former USSR, relying upon two indicators:

- the average value of the conflict potential for all ethnic areas;
- the average level of political mobilisation of minorities in their areas.

Table 2 shows that the highest conflict potential manifests itself in those FSU republics where, strange as it may seem, fighting has not yet started i.e., in the area of the Russian (Russian speaking) population in Estonia – the only such area in that country, but which is able to guarantee its status of the largest ethnic area due to the great number of people and its share in the state's and area's population. This area

---

9 Kolossov, V. and R. Turovskii. "Tak li uzh grozen Groznyi? [Is Groznyi Really so Terrible?]" *Novoe vremya* 1993, no. 11: 42-43; Kolossov, V.A. "Narod ne bezmolstvuet, no vprok li urok? [The People Do Not Keep Silent. But Is the Lesson Learnt?]" *Rossiiskaya federatsiya* 1994, no. 3: 13-15.

also enjoys the most advanced geopolitical and economic position (e.g., the Estonian periphery, which badly needs reconstruction, was left by the national authorities to drift in the 'rough seas' of the market when all traditional links have been totally disrupted). At the same time, the political mobilisation of the non-titular majority in north-east Estonia is as yet not very high, which provides hopes for a peaceful solution of the conflict if equal political rights are granted to both the 'natives' 'and non-natives'.

It is Russia's good luck that the most acute ethnic conflicts have not reached its territory so far, except for the conflict between Ossetians and Ingush people. The average of ethnic and political tension is much lower than in other FSU countries in general: 10.6 against 13.2. Nevertheless, this is of little consolation, if one takes into account the numerous smouldering conflicts and the acuteness of the situation in the areas populated by Russians along the borders.

On the whole, the highest conflict potential is naturally demonstrated by those FSU states where military confrontation or civil war have already been unleashed – Tadzhikistan, Azerbaidzhan, Georgia, Moldova, with exceptions being Latvia and Lithuania, again due to the geopolitical position of their ethnic areas, their concentration and the clear-cut difference between their culture and that of the titular nationality. Yet even in these cases, unlike in the Transcaucasian republics, Tadzhikistan and Moldova, political mobilisation in ethnic areas is low. Among other CIS states, Ukraine and Uzbekistan have 'scored' comparatively highly: the former – due to the geopolitical position of its heavily populated ethnic areas; the latter – because of cultural and historical factors.

Within the republics the ethno-political tension index goes far above the FSU average in the 'old' areas of ethno-political tension, such as Abkhazia, Nagorno Karabakh, Chechnya, Ossetia and Ingushetia; Gorny Badakhshan and the Uzbek areas in Tadzhikistan, where a high level of political mobilisation keeps conflicts 'glowing'. Potentially the most dangerous situation is in Tuva, in many areas populated by Russians in the Baltic countries, Moldova and the Crimea (here a Crimean Tatar area is gaining power); although the ethno-political mobilisation of minorities there is either low or medium-high, except for the Crimea. Somewhat lower is the tension index in the large Tatar and Baskhir areas in Russia and Yakutia, although the level of political mobilisation is increasing there. The whole of the North Caucasus (and not only its central and southern parts) is an area of total ethnic conflict danger. In the ethnic areas of the Karachaev, Cherkes, Balkar, Kabardin and

Dagestan peoples the overall index of tension is coupled with the high level of nationally grounded political mobilisation.

In the four main areas of Cossack population in Russia the whole complex of parameters comes close to the all-Russian average. However, the level of political mobilisation here is comparatively high, and may indeed rise unexpectedly. V. Petukhov, chief of the Rostov *oblast'* administration's department on Cossacks' affairs, stated that if 'signing up with the Cossacks' becomes beneficial then their number in the *oblast'* will leap from the current figure (estimated by local experts) up to 1 million people. Cossack organisations are strictly disciplined and their leaders may organise a rally overnight in the comparatively small Novocherkassk of 30-40,000 seriously minded men in uniform, that may only outwardly appear histrionic (as happened during the events of October 1993).

5 Ethnic Areas in the European Part of the FSU against a European Background

It is well-known that the border between Western and Eastern Europe can be drawn by using many different criteria: geopolitical – that is, between the former socialist and the rest of the countries; cultural and geographic – between western and eastern Christian states (in which case the Baltic states, most part of Central Europe, Slovenia and Croatia will join the western Christian world, whereas Greece, on the contrary, will find itself in the eastern Christian block). Yet, no matter what criteria we may use, the share of national minorities in their areas in the population of three main parts of Europe (West, East, the FSU – together or without the Baltic states, but including Transcaucasus) will be rather similar – ranging from 10% to 15%, i.e., it will be slightly lower in Western Europe and slightly higher in the former USSR. Yugoslavia presents a striking exception, where the 'area-type' minorities used to comprise 36.5% of the population.

Minorities in the ethnic areas of the European territories of the FSU are, on the average, smaller than those in Western and Eastern Europe (1.00, 1.12 and 1.08 points respectively). Their share is smaller in the overall population of these states (0.24, 0.36 and 0.50) and in the population of the corresponding political and administrative areas (0.92, 1.21 and 1.11). The absolute strength of such minorities in the European part of the former USSR and in Western Europe is quite similar – 31.3 and 35.7 million people. However, the ethno-political situation in Eastern Europe is certainly a good deal more acute than in the West, though there are some 'hot spots' there too. Strange as it may seem, and, again, no matter how we define borders between the sub-continents, the general ethno-political situation in Eastern Europe is much worse than it is in the former USSR. The reason for this is the crisis in Yugoslavia, other Balkan areas and Romania.

General indexes of ethnic tension are: in Western Europe – 11.31; in Eastern Europe – 14.83 (in the former Yugoslavia – 16.13); in the European territories of the former USSR – 13.24. However, the 'hottest spots' in the former USSR can compare only to those in Yugoslavia, although the abundance of ethnic areas (primarily in Russia) balances the picture. It should be especially noted that it is the former Soviet Union that leads in the average political mobilisation of ethnic groups in their areas, yielding only to Yugoslavia.

Apart from political mobilisation, other components of ethno-political tension in Eastern Europe rank higher than in the West and in the European part of the former USSR. Naturally, the economic factors of ethno-political risk are more significant in the West of Europe than in the East, whereas in the former socialist countries the self-identification of minorities in their areas plays a more important role. The latter is closely connected with the struggle for preservation, the everyday use and official status of the minority's mother tongue and also with religious discrepancies. Moreover, it is highly important that Western European minorities in their areas are 'old', and have long since adapted themselves to coexistence with the titulary nations of the states (a minority's average 'age' is estimated in the West at 0.07 points, in the East – 0.61, and in the European territory of the former USSR – 0.26). National minorities in ethnic areas of the West have far more rarely enjoyed statehood than those in Eastern Europe (with the exception of Russia).

To sum up, the objective grounds for national conflicts in the ethnic areas of Russia are not as dramatic as one might think them to be in the current critical situation. The disintegration of the Russian Federation along the lines of its ethnic areas is not necessarily inevitable. In Western Europe the situation, according to many parameters, is comparable but there it has been possible so far to maintain a relatively low level of political mobilisation of minorities in their areas. As for Russia, there are certainly real 'hot spots' there, first and foremost, in the North Caucasus. Russia cannot disengage itself from the situation in the Russian-speaking areas in the countries of the 'near abroad' – areas that are the largest in Europe in terms of their population and that have a highly explosive potential.

Only a comparatively low level of political mobilisation prevents a dangerous aggravation of the situation there, yet the Crimean experience demonstrates that political indifference is far from being an imminent feature of Russian-speaking minorities. The national-territorial principle of state structure is the most powerful mine, laid by the communist regime under the unity of Russia. It increases geopolitical risk many times. Obviously, it is hardly possible to do away with this risk at the drop of a hat; any attempts to do so will cause strong opposition and painful conflicts. It seems more prudent to increase the competence of the subjects of the federation and to stimulate creation of territorial associations that would traverse ethnic borders in order to solve economic, cultural, ecological and other problems. Such measures would allow, after a while, to avoid the present-day absolutisation of national and territorial borders in all spheres of life.

9

Present-Day National and Inter-Ethnic Relations in the Republic of Belarus

Igor' Chakvin and Tadeush Novogrodskii

1 Introduction

The present report deals with current national and inter-ethnic relations in the Republic of Belarus (RB) and analyses the major tendencies of their development today and in the nearest future. The development of national, inter-national, and inter-ethnic processes is of the utmost importance to today's Belarus, and in a number of cases these processes even transcend national borders and affect neighbouring states and ethnic groups. The study of these relations is also prompted by the following elements:

- the geographical position of Belarus which finds itself sandwiched 'between East and West';
- the various clearly expressed outward political orientations of the major social elite groups, movements and parties; and
- the historical and ethno-genetic peculiarities of population in different regions of Belarus.

The present study also deals with problems of national policies in Belarus, main national doctrines, the role of the 'nation' in the post-Soviet period which is characterised by the absence of one dominant social and state ideology. The current irreconcilability of nationalist and internationalist points of view on the future development of the Belarus nation is not conducive to the consolidation of society, neither does it help to reach political national and inter-ethnic stability. On the other hand, the ideas of national revival in newly independent Belarus find a limited number of supporters among the de-nationalised Russified and Polonised population that lacks its own national identity.

The national consolidation of society in Belarus is also hampered by the clearly emerging divergent religious orientation among a considerable number of people in

Belarus (with Catholics and Orthodox Christians contending for supremacy). This creates an atmosphere of cultural and religious alienation, a feeling of falling behind vis-à-vis the neighbouring nations. In a poly-ethnic state where alongside ethnic Belarussians there live large ethnic groups of Russians, Ukrainians, Poles, Tatars and others, all these processes continue to develop and are felt both at the individual and group level creating specific conditions of inter-ethnic relations.

The above-mentioned tendencies and processes have been analysed to be used as an information basis for the present report. Numerous other sources have also been used: ethno-sociological studies; statistical materials dealing with ethnic (national) and quantitative make-up of the population; result of ethnographic surveys and interviews; scholarly studies and materials appearing in the press; different party programs; sociological public opinion polls carried out by the Belarus *Obshchestvennoe Mnenie* [Public Opinion] Service; by the institute of Sociology of the Academy of Science of Belarus, by the Independent Institute of Social Economic and Political Studies; public addresses of political and party leaders; and some radio and TV broadcasts that were aired in 1994 and 1995.

In characterising national peculiarities and the concepts of 'nation', 'ethnos', 'ethnicity', and 'nationality', both local (V.U. Promley, V. Tishkov and others) and foreign (D. White, A. Smith, A. Cobban, E. Gellner) terminology and methodology to be found in scholarly works have been used in the present study[1]. Also a number of concepts, developed by D. Campbell, R. Levine and D. Bell have been borrowed for the needs of the present study (with corresponding references make in the text). In this report we mean by 'national relations' all the processes, relations, and phenomena which contribute to the formation and development of ethnic or national communities, in our particular case that of the Belarus nation. By 'inter-ethnic relations'[2] we mean contact of groups or individuals belonging to different ethnoses within the framework of the national state of Belarus; by 'inter-national relations' we mean contacts at the inter-state level, or between people of different nationalities.

---

1 Bronilei, Yu. *Ocherki teorii etnosa*. Moscow, 1983; Tishkov, V. „Etnichnost' i Vlast' v SSSR." *Sovetskaya etnografiya* 1993, no. 3; White, Philip. „What is a nationality?" *Canadian Review of Studies in Nationalism* 12 (1985), no. 1; Smith, Anthony. *The Ethnic Origins of Nations*. Oxford, 1988; Cobban, A. *The National State and National Self-Determinations*. New York, 1970; Gellner, E. „Ethnicity and Faith in Eastern Europe." *Daedalus* 119 (1990).

2 In Soviet and post-Soviet literature these relations are incorrectly defined as inter-national.

2 Main Doctrines and Concepts of National Development in Belarus

The development of national relations in the process of creating a new Belarus state and the emergence of a new social-political community in the Republic of Belarus (RB) has been for some time the focus of attention not only in Belarus but also in some circles of the European public, of scholars and politicians. But neither the Belarus authorities nor major parties and political movements have been able to work out large-scale state-level programs, let alone to put them into practice. One can say that there is no state policy in the sphere of national relations at all. With a few exceptions, such a clearly defined policy is absent from the programs of most of the political parties which are careful not to aggravate the situation in national relations. In many cases they do not bother to study these relations in order to understand them better.

To a certain extent the program of the Belarussian Popular Front (BPF)[3] is one of these exceptions. The BPF program is based on the doctrine of ethno-nationalism, according to which a people-nation as a specific ethnic community, initially has a historical right to have its 'own' national state and this right makes its existence legitimate.

This incites a drive towards constant consolidation of the ethnic nucleus of a nation on the basis of its linguistic, cultural and mental identification which, as a rule in a poly-ethnic state deepens the division between 'we' and 'they' and thus creates a certain nationally inspired situation that is ripe with conflict.

The BPF ethno-national doctrine is shared completely or in part by a number of other parties, namely: the National-Democratic Party of Belarus (NDPB)[4]; the Belarussian Social-Democratic Gromada (BSDG); the United Democratic Party of Belarus (UDPB); the Belarussian Christian Democratic Union (BCDU); the Party of Popular Concord (PPC) and others, which also stand for the priority of the rights of the individual over the rights of the state or the nation rights, for the rights of national (ethnic) minorities and others similar issues. Conceptually these program points transform the idea of an ethnic-national state orientation into an idea of recognising a nation as a political and poly-ethnic formation in which the ethnic features marking the ethnic identity (for example language), symbols and values of the Belarussians are nevertheless generally accepted and predominant.

---

3 The Program of the Belarussian Popular Front: 6 Minsk: Independent State – *Adradzhan'nye*', 1993.

4 In recent times the word 'Belarus' is not officially used in the name of the Party.

The majority of the Belarus population possessing the Belarus ethnic identity treats these ideas with indifference or has no knowledge of them. They are far more commonly known and upheld among political elites, patriotically and nationalistically oriented groups of population such as students, people with the highest level of education (scholars, scientists, writers and other intellectuals), and educators.

At the same time the anti-Communist and anti-imperial position of the Belarussian Popular Front (BPF), the massive popular rallies that are organised by the BPF and other affiliated parties to expose the repressions of the Stalin period and rehabilitate of victims of bolshevik terror, the *Mortirolog* movement, the support of those who have been badly affected by the Chernobyl disaster etc. - all of these things attract a lot of supporters to the general and not only the nationalities program of the BPF. That is why the number of people who support the general BPF programs or share their ideas is quite representative and makes up (according to different estimates) between 12 and 20 per cent of the electorate. Supporters of these programs are to found in all strata of society and geographically practically in all areas of Belarus and its major towns (Minsk, Vitebsk, Mogylev, Grodno, Gomel'', Brest, Polotsk, Solygorsk, Molodecho, Ivatsevych and others). The BPF has representations outside Belarus in Moscow, Riga, Vilnius, Poland, USA and Canada[5].

The general programs of the BPF and other parties that are similar in their views on national state development in Belarus are opposed by numerous but small political parties and movements which, as a rule, do not have a unified national program. Among them those of pro-communist and pro-imperial leaning: the Party of Communists of Belarus (PCB), the Union of Veterans, the Slavonic Sobor [Community], *Belaya Rus'*, the Union of Officers, the Movement for Democracy, Social Progress and Justice, to name a just few.

To a great extent these movements, organisations, and parties are made up of former Soviet, Communist Party, and Young Communist League functionaries (mostly from the top echelons of their hierarchies), managers of large factories and of kolkhozes [collective farms], veterans and pensioners, retired officers of the Soviet Armed Forces, immigrants from Russia and Ukraine, and also those who

---

5 BPF is from 5,000 to 15,000 strong but these include only active party functionaries. Political parties and social-political movements of Belarus. Minsk, 1993.

made it big at the state level of the former USSR[6]. These political movements and parties share a common set of ideas which revolve around weakening and doing away altogether with Belarus' independence, which hinders the re-establishment of the USSR or the creation of a new Union of Slavic peoples under the aegis of Russia (or a Euro-Asian Union, including Kazakhstan). Within the framework of such programs one can find ideas of creating a poly-ethnic civil-state nation (Smith 1988) with the Russian language being used as an official state language, with Orthodox Christianity as a prevailing faith, etc.

Members of these organisations and parties are politically active and socially influential, they enjoy quite broad support from outside the country – mostly from Russia and to a lesser extent from Ukraine (among the supporters one can find official, political and cultural figures, mass media etc.). Some polls show that they enjoy the support of about 20 per cent of potential electors.

For the time being, the ideals expressed by members of these pro-communist and pro-imperial organisations and parties and their activities do not find wide support in Belarussian society at large, which tends to be generally indifferent to both these and other ideologies. But in some Eastern areas of Belarus with larger numbers of supporters of these ideas, numerous inter-national conflict situations are a frequent occurrence[7]. As a rule these conflict situations are provoked by extremists of pro-Russian, pro-imperial and even pro-communist leanings. Branches of the *Russian National Unity* party in Belarus, the Liberal-Democratic Party of Belarus, national-communist groupings (of the *Krasnyi Marsh* [Red March] kind), militant (in spite of their small numbers) organisations of Belarussian Cossacks, unions of army officers and veterans and other similar organisations are very active in promoting pro-communist and imperial ideas. The radicalisation of nationalist and patriotic groupings (made up mostly of young people) within the BPF and outside it (for example within the Belarussian nationalist organisation *Pravyi Revansh* [Rightist Revenge]) may by regarded as a natural reaction to pro-communist and imperial militants.

The conflicting sides resort to different means of fighting each other and try to increase their influence in the electorate, mass media, and parliament.

---

6 The number of supporters of these parties as smaller than those of other parties. „We and Time." (Minsk), no. 22 , 1993.

7 A similar situation in found in and around Vitebsk where local authorities (mostly made up of former communist-party functionaries) early on an openly anti-national and often enough – anti-state policies.

These two opposing party groups represent two major poles on the political spectrum of society in their attitudes both to national relations and state independence. The major part of society holds centrist, neutral, or liberal opinions (which are reflected in the ideological precepts of a number of parties such as PPC, BSDG, BCP). But sociological surveys and polls show a considerable number of respondents who have little or no knowledge of these parties' programmes[8] .

The position of parliament and of high officials can be described as not having any clear-cut national-state doctrine. In fact, it finds itself under the influence of different politicised groupings and movements, parties and organisations. The problem becomes especially acute because the citizens do not express any clear-cut views with respect to the national, political, legal and economic make-up of the country and do not seem particularly inclined to achieve anything concrete in these spheres. The Belarussian society at large is at the moment mainly oriented towards economic survival. Politically the society is demoralised, socially it is fragmented, and nationally it is amorphous. The weakness of the political elites and the absence of a stable middle class make it impossible to effectively oppose any forms of dictatorial actions on the part of the executive power and the authoritarian forms it takes.

Some events of the recent years connected with dismissal of a number of state leaders (S. Shushkevich, V. Kebich, A. Lukashenko) have provided ample proof of that: the external and internal geopolitical orientations of these leaders lied at the basis of the official position of Belarus in the sphere of national policies. For Belarussian state independence the question was „To be or not to be“, and consequently it had to be decided whether to support the independent development of the Belarussian nation as a single state-social body, or to let the ethnic nation[9] of Belarussians join a bigger national-political formation, namely Russia, preserving only a limited measure of federal autonomy. It has not been yet decided which road the country will follow. That is why the declaration of state sovereignty – a constitutionally proclaimed concept of national status – remains a formal proclamation. In fact, the realisation of this concept is not taking place because society lacks the mechanisms (certain social forces, national concord, a common will

---

8 Karbalevich, V., V. Lomako, G. Pashkovskii, V. Stupnikov. *Development of Multiparty System in Belarus*. Minsk: 'Vostok-Zapad', 1994: 14-15, 35.

9 Definitions and classifications of types of national groups and communities have been taken from: Smith, Anthony. *The Ethnic Origins of Nations*. Oxford, 1988; Cobbon, A. *The National State and National Self-Determination*. New York, 1970.

etc.) that would set it in motion, and also because there are certain factors that prevent it. These factors are worth to be dealt with in greater detail.

2.1 Factors Determining Inter-Ethnic Relations

The factors which determine national and inter-ethnic relations in Belarus today have come to the fore after the collapse of the Soviet Union: the political situation changed radically and the Belarussian Soviet Socialist Republic gained independence and became the Republic of Belarus. The newly gained sovereignty posed many questions, one of them being: what kind of state was to be built in Belarus? It would be extremely difficult to adapt the western type of democratic state to local conditions, because the former local conditions with firmly ingrained and virtually unchanged Soviet and socialist traditions remained in place. Nevertheless a complex mixture gradually came into being of old socialist political institutions combined with new post-Soviet and Western ones which allowed the mechanism of power to function in a relatively stable way. This power had retained its status with a state, national and Belarussian character. This is how a future form of the national state formation can be defined, based on the type of a number of national political communities in the West[10].

But the gradual democratisation of society, the growth of the population's social activity and, most importantly, the sharp upsurge of ethno-national self consciousness (i.e. a growing search of Belarussians for their national identity), produced in the Belarussians a new understanding of what the Belarus nation should be. In the opinion of many it is an ethnos with its own statehood within the system of which representatives of other nations and nationalities can live – and have Belarus citizenship[11]. There also exists another understanding of what a nation should be. This understanding views a nation as an ethnic community whose representatives have a common ancestry, history, territory and share the same language, same traditions and culture, same ethnic identity, including self-identification, mentality

---

10 Primarily in Britain, France, USA where the an old law 'ius soli' (the law of the soil') is still retained and a nation is understood as a political-territorial civic society.

11 Here, characteristic is a sharp reaction on the part of a number of pro-russian organizations to the celebrations commemorating the anniversary of the Orsha battle in 1514, when the Belarussian and Lithuanian troops defeated a Moscow army the Russian Ambassador to Belarus, I. Saprykin, commenting on the 200th anniversary celebrations devoted to T. Kostyusko uprising, said that 'the whole thing smacks of Russophobia'.

and psychological features). This view of 'nation' is prevalent in certain other European countries.[12]

The heightened activity of society's ethno-national movements has brought the question about the role and place of the Belarussian language to the fore. The Belarussian language has acquired a constitutional status as Belarus' state language (parliament passed a special law dealing with the language situation in the country). There were instances of the Belarussian language being introduced almost by force, but in all cases it came to be regarded as either mandatory or highly desirable in all official transactions. It is compulsory to study the Belarussian language in secondary schools, to use it in official clerical work and official transactions, in radio and TV broadcasts; and it is desirable to use it in higher educational establishments in general and in liberal arts colleges in particular, in book publishing, periodicals etc.

The national language, no doubt, should receive a lot of attention from the state and society but in 'civilised' countries this is done through academies of sciences, poets and writers, translations, dictionaries, TV and radio broadcasts, national schools which students attend voluntarily rather than under pressure from the state[13]. Unfortunately at the official state level, the deeply engrained Soviet bureaucratic attitude towards problem-solving has led to complications in putting the programmes of introducing the Belarussian language into all spheres of life into practice[14].

The Belarussian society that had either partially forgotten the Belarussian language, or had never known it in the first place, reacted against the attempts to introduce the language into all spheres of life in various ways. Gradually there emerged stable groups of those who were in favour of it and those who were against it, with the majority of population remaining vastly indifferent and preferring to speak a sub-literary mixture of Russian and Belarussian dialects (the two basic types of local vernacular are called *setchka* and *trasyanka*).

---

12 For example Germans prefer to keep to the ancient roman tradition regarding 'soobshchestvo' ('community') primarily as 'Jus sanguinis' (Literally: 'the law of blood'); See White, Philip L. „What is a nationality?" *Canadian Review of Studies in Nationalism* 12 (1985), no. 1.

13 The *Tavarystvo Belarskay Movy Imya T. Skaryny* non-profit society in Belarus has been active in spreading the Belarussian language and this example should be studied and emulated

14 The role of bureaucracy in the process of shaping a nation is ambivalent greatest successes in these processes the bureaucratic method of uniting and unifying a nation, a state etc. is usually achieved under the totalitarian and autocratic forms of government. Under the conditions of democratic changes taking place in Belarus, the russianized Belarussian bureaucracy did not play the role it used to under totalitarianism.

Further attempts were made to give an ethnic character to the Belarussian statehood through the introduction of a new state coat-of-arms and new insignia, Belarussian money, The 'Belarussification' of the armed forces, new national history and mentality, etc. The attempts, which were made both at the state level through parliament, executive power, scholarly and popular publications, and at the level of literature, groupings, language-and-culture societies, only made the national problem in Belarus even more acute.

A number of groups within the Belarus population has developed imperial, pro-Russian, pro-soviet and also nationalist but not pro-Belarussian leanings. A considerable number of people also show nihilistic attitudes towards Belarus national statehood. The hopeless economic policies that are carried out by the government greatly contribute this kind of nihilism. Among other contributing factors one can name the government's pro-Russian geopolitical orientations, the higher living standards of neighbouring nations (Russia, Lithuania and Latvia), and the provincialism in a number of different spheres: in local culture, science, literature, arts. It is very characteristic that the number of migrants from the Baltic states to Belarus have dropped considerably in recent years, in spite of the fact that ethnic Belarussians experience difficulties in getting themselves naturalised there. The economic factor also to a great extent influences intern-national relations, attitudes and views, particularly at the grass-roots level (where attitudes of the following kind are widely spread: „Give us a lot of cheap food and then we'll talk Belarussian").

Negative trends in the economy of Belarus are currently one of the destabilising factors not only in the general social but also in the national sense. The struggle for survival and the all-pervading pragmatism considerably 'neutralise' the national idea, make it of little interest to the majority of Belarus' population. Only a limited number of people share the view that ethno-national consolidation will contribute to economic stability and lead to accelerated development. No more than 10 to 15 per cent of the population believe that the living standards will probably go up if the BPF will come to power and although the number of BPF supporters is gradually growing, there is no wide social basis for nationalism[15] in Belarus yet.

The spreading of nationalism is also hindered by ethno-genetic, religious, mental, and other factors. Thus, a considerable number of Belarussians connect their

---

15 The term 'nationalism' in this essay is used in the sense usually used in the West that is meaning 'an intense national feeling'; see: Gellner, E. „Ethnicity and Faith in Eastern Europe." *Daedalus* 119 (1990), no. 1.

ethnicity (*Belaruskost'* [Belarussianess]) with the fact of having been born on the territory of Belarus and having parents who have been registered (one of the parents, or both) as 'Belarussians'. Current public opinion polls and ethnographic data show that these factors have been the leading ones in ethnic self-identification and self-appellation for the majority of Belarussians. To a lesser extent the population recognises the common background of ancestry, language, culture, traditions as uniting factors. This somewhat weakened recognition of one's ethnic background (ethnic identity) can be explained by certain peculiarities in the ethnogenesis of people, by the multiplicity of self-identifications that was to be found in Belarus as late as the end of the 20th century (certain groups of Belarussian population called themselves '*rus'kie*', '*litsviny*', '*poleshchuky*', to name a few), which has affected the processes of ethno-national consolidation.[16]

To a great extent the ethno-genetic factor determines the particularities of national consolidation at present as well. Thus for some territorial (Eastern and Southern) groups of Belarussians, ethic identification with neighbours (Russians, Ukrainians) sometimes prevails over ethnicity identification with other, for example Western groups of Belarussians. The 'dividing' factor is often enough a different religious affiliation (Orthodox Christians and Catholics), while the uniting factor combines in itself a common self-identification, common territory, common history, common country of origin. But in spite of the tendency to be easily assimilated (Russified), Belarussians in general tend to steadily keep their ethnic label for quite a long time even outside Belarus (thus according to the census of 1989 1.2 mln. people in Russia alone referred to themselves as 'Belarussians').

In spite of the fact that the majority of the Belarussian population speaks Russian, about 60 per cent of Belarussians consider the Belarussian language to be their second language.

2.2 Ethnocentrist and national revival trends

Today there are about 8 million Belarussians living in Belarus, and these make op about 78 per cent of the entire population. The Belarussians can be described as a nation (according to the typology developed by A. Smith it is 'an ethnic nation') with a fully-developed social structure that is characteristic of an industrial society

---

16 Chakvin, T. and P. Tereshkovich. „Iz Istoryy stanovlenyya natsional'nogo soznaniya belorussov (XIX–nachalo XX v). [From the history of development of national self-consciousness of Belarussians', 19 th.–early 20 th. century]." *Sovetskaya Etnografiya* 1990, no. 6: 43, 49-50.

and with its own statehood. Despite unfavourable social and economic conditions and a high level of assimilation (mostly Russification), the majority of the Belarussians in general and the agrarian population in particular have preserved their ethno-cultural futures and identity.

In the years of Soviet power, the Belarussians had come to regard Belarus as their 'own' national state with its 'own' political elite (regardless of the fact that this elite was devoid of any real power). Today, new political and intellectual elites use different ways of resisting any attempts to change the status of Belarus or even to abolish its independence. Society is being constantly supplied with ideas of 'national revival'[17] and of strengthening national statehood through achieving true sovereignty as one of the European states.

These ideas find currency not only in the nationally oriented, radical groups of society but also in liberal ones, among intellectuals and even among state officials at certain levels of the power hierarchy. V. Danilenko, Belarussian Ambassador to the Russian Federation, believes that Belarus has already chosen its own 'Belarussian way' both in politics and in economics and that in today's geopolitical structures Belarus plays a leading role in helping to maintain the precarious balance between West and East.[18]

These ideas are extremely popular among the Belarussian diaspora, representatives of which from the former Republics of the former Soviet Union, Poland, Great Britain, USA, Canada and other countries have set up the *Bats'kavshchyna* [Motherland] Association of Belarussians of the World[19].

Branches of the *Bats'kavshchyna* association have been set up in regional centres and major town of Belarus and elsewhere. The association aims to contribute to the revival of culture, language, national self-consciousness and traditions of the Belarussian people; to promote consolidation and unification of the Belarussians of the whole world regardless of their party affiliations, political views, social and economic position, religious affiliation; and to further beneficial relations of Belarus with foreign countries. It should be noted that these aims in many respects

---

17 This term implies the revival of such national features (language, culture, traditions, statehood) which were characteristic of the Belarussians in the best periods of their ethnic history, namely in the 14 th. – 18 th. century in the 20 s and 30 s of the 20 Th. century; *Entsyklopediya historyyi Belarusi* [Encyclopaedia of History of Belarus]. Minsk, 1993. Vol. 1: 58-61.

18 *Belaruskaya minuyshchina* 1993, no. 2: 32.

19 The Belarussian Diaspora all around the world is estimated to be between one and two million people.

correspond to the tasks declared in the programs of many political parties and movements in Belarus.

The upsurge of national feelings among the Belarussian diaspora is reflected in a similar tendency within Belarus itself. This tendency involves mostly young people, students, and intellectuals who show a stable trend towards national ethnocentrism[20]. Ethnocentric tendencies coincide with attempts to revive the 'typically Belarussian religions' of the Unite church (the so-called Greek-Catholic Church) and paganism and (to a lesser degree) with attempts to 'Belarussianise' the orthodox and catholic churches in Belarus. Ethnocentrism is particularly noticeable in the cultural life of Belarus, in scholarly publications, in radio and TV broadcasts, and in the new 'national' holidays and memorial days that are being constantly introduced.

Its should be noted that in contrast to the Russians, the majority of Belarussians do not associate the national idea with *sobornost'* ('unification, conciliarism' and more all rolled into one term), with sacramental autocracy (with the exception here of the hard-core communists), with Christian Orthodoxy or with missionary activities among non-believers. Ideas of national unification of the Belarussians are based on simplified anti-Russian and anti-polish feelings which are backed by critical attitudes towards concepts like 'Great Russia', 'Great Poland' or 'Soviet Internationalism'. Ethnocentrism, 'return to ethnicity', and nationalism are no doubt contributing to the aggravation of inter-ethnic and inter-national relations. But these processes in Belarus can be described as being latent and do not significantly affect the general trends in politics because of the small number of their supporters.

Ethnocentric tendencies acquire peculiar forms at the grass-roots level, especially on the countryside. Many inhabitants of the rural areas, in an attempt to uphold their national identity, ascribe to their ethnic neighbours negative features (which in fact they possess themselves), while regarding their 'own' local ethnographic features of culture, everyday life, psychology, dialect, etc. as superior. When such attitudes coincide with differences in religious affiliations, this tendency grows stronger but still not does not dominate in inter-group relations.

Similar processes are taking place over wider geographical and social areas, for example in the western and eastern parts of Belarus, where due to historical factors rather peculiar ethnic (ethnographic) features have developed. The ethno-psychology

---

20 In this case, ethnocentrism, as an idea of superiority of one's own ethnos (ethnic group) over others, is understood along the lines set by D. Campbell and R. Levine, and also D. Bell. See: Campbell, D. and R. Levine. *Ethnocentrism. Theories of Conflict, Ethnic Attitudes and Group Behavior*. New York, 1972: 1-2; Bell, Daniel. „Ethnicity and Social Change." In *Ethnicity Theory and Experience*. Cambridge, Mass., 1975: 144-147; 171-174.

of 'westerners' (i.e. those, who live in the west of Belarus), either Catholics and Orthodox Christians, can be described as being more oriented towards ethnocentrism than that of the inhabitants of Belarus' eastern parts. It should be mentioned that a similar situation of 'new tribalism' can be detected among natives of western Belarus who ethnically are not Belarussians but Poles, Russians, Tatars, Ukrainians and others.

But these natural national feelings in today's Belarus have not reached the level where they lead to animosity and conflicts. This is the way it has been in the historically observable past and the way tends to remain today, as long as different national backgrounds do not become a reason for starting a struggle for survival with other competing groups, or for getting an advantageous position in society in general and in governing bodies in particular. Although these negative phenomena (anti-Semitism, russophobia, polonophobia) can be found at the level of everyday contacts they do not constitute any major trend in the ethnic processes of today's Belarus.[21] The Belarussian society is generally devoid of an 'enemy image' or of a desire to find fault with neighbouring nations, minority ethnic groups and foreigners and to blame them for whatever hardships the country may be experiencing.[22]

All this can be regarded as evidence that ethnocentrism and nationalism in Belarus are not very pronounced among the majority of population and are only weakly conflict-stimulating; neither are they filled with an excessively developed irrational element that causes so much trouble in inter-national and inter-ethnic relations.

Character and Peculiarities of Inter-Ethnic Relations

Belarus is a poly-ethnic state where many ethnic groups live alongside the Belarussians. The second biggest ethnic group after the Belarussians are the Russians with 1.3 mln. or about 12 percent of the entire population. The number of Russians (*Velikorossy* [Great Russians]) has grown in recent decades due to the migration into Belarus of workers, servicemen, teachers and college instructors, scholars and scientists. There is also a considerable number of ethnic Russians in Belarus whose ancestors moved to Belarus a long time age (for example, there are more than 100,000 *staroobryadtsy* – adherents of old style Orthodox Christianity),

---

21 Ibidem.

22 Feeble attempts at 'dehumanization' of the image of a neighboring nation are made by some Belarussian national-fundamentalists, mostly when they try to re-assess the historical past of the Belarussian, Russian and Polish peoples and to create a new nationalist mythology.

among them tsarist-time officials and intellectuals. They are scattered more or less evenly across the Belarussian territory and there are no clearly defined enclaves, although most ethnic Russians are concentrated in the eastern areas of Belarus (Vitebsk *oblast'*, Mogilev *oblast'*, Gomel' *oblast'*) as well as in the capital and major industrial cities where only recently they represented up to 20 per cent of the population[23].

The prevailing majority of ethnic Russians (with the exception of the *staroobryadtsy*) has become culturally and otherwise assimilated into the Belarussian ethnic environment, but they continue to preserve their self-identification, their self-consciousness, their language, and their religion. The main features they want to retain as their ethnic self-identification are their common ancestry, language and religion, and the 'Russian faith', in other words Orthodox Christianity[24]. 'Great Russian' chauvinism manifests itself only in a small number of people, and is mostly confined to retired servicemen, and other pro-Russian politicised groups. Migrations from Belarus to Russia have grown in recent years and are motivated primarily by economic and not by national or religious reasons.

Close ethno-genetic roots and a common history that dates back to the end of the 18th century have determined the character of inter-ethnic relations with the natives and these relations have for the most part been peaceful and friendly. The closeness of the Russian and Belarussian languages, the mutual cultural assimilation (Russians were 'belarussified', and Belarussians were Russified), and later the 'Sovietisation' of all ethnic groups were among the factors that contributed to peaceful relations. The dominant position of the Russian language and culture for a long time has been an assimilating factor, involving considerable numbers of native Belarussians, mostly in urban areas and Orthodox Christians, who gradually changed their ethnic self-identification or accepted a double self-identification and considered themselves simultaneously both Russians and Belarussians in culture, self-consciousness and religion[25].

---

23 *Etnicheskie protsessy i obraz zhizni* [Ethnical processes and Way of Life]. Minsk: 24-27.

24 Up to 1917 all throughout Belarus and up to 1933 in Western Belarus, notions 'Orthodox Christian' and 'Russian' (or as a variant 'Belarussian') were treated as identical and used as synonyms

25 The idea of close ethnic kinship of Russians and Belarussians (and also Ukrainians) was supported in the USSR not only at the governmental level also in scientific and fictional literature and in the official concept, launched in the 60's of 'the flourishing, drawing closer together and merging of all the peoples of the USSR into one nation' it was envisioned that the first in this process were to be Russians and Belarussians.

Changes of ethnic self-identification were especially popular among the Belarussians in the post-World War II years. By the mid-50s this process had acquired such proportions that the authorities feared it might get out of control and decided to curb it by registering the nationality in internal passports with the nationality of only parent being taken into account. The official statistics of the post-Stalin period were trimmed to show only the growth and not the reduction in number of 'the Soviet Socialist' nations. Since then the Russians population in Belarus has been increasing mostly through natural growth (inter-ethnic marriages) and migration. Today those groups and families of the Belarussian population that have been completely assimilated (in other words those who have changed their self-identification) do not show (neither do ethnic Russians who have retained their ethnicity) any striving to separatism, but it is among them that tendencies of internationalism, nihilistic attitudes towards the Belarussians statehood and language, and a desire for political consolidation and re-unification with Russia are to be found.

The ethnic Russians of Belarus have all the social, political and national possibilities for satisfying their ethnic cultural and language needs. Today in Belarus one can find Moscow periodicals, local Russian-language newspapers, functioning Russian language theatres, Russian high schools and colleges. A considerable amount of airtime is given to Russian-language TV and radio broadcasts. Mutual activities of the Belarussian branch of the Russian Orthodox Church and the Moscow Patriarchy which are aimed at further consolidating Russian and Belarussian Orthodox Christians receive wide coverage in the mass media. Branches of Russian nationalist parities and movements (*Slavyanskii Sobor*, *Rus'*, Liberal-Democratic Party of Russia and others) are functioning in Belarus.

The main problem in inter-ethnic relations between Russians and Belarussians is the language one (the problem of bilingualism). This problem arose after Belarussian had been introduced in the majority of schools in Belarus (over 90%) as the language of instruction. The majority of the Belarussian population show understanding on this issue or remain non-committed. The problem is aggravated by the fact that a considerable number of native Belarussians think that the Belarussian language has no future, that it is the language of the poorly-educated rural population and call for the Russian language to be introduced as a 'state language' alongside Belarussian.

The language problem is periodically complicated by the conflict-provoking actions of Belarussian nationalist radicals and chauvinist imperial (pro-Russian) politicised groups of society; by somewhat strained relations between Belarus and Russian Federation at the government level (delayed payments, disruption in supplies, particularly of energy sources, geopolitical attitudes of Russia towards Belarus); by the processes of 'Belarussification' and national revival which entail a re-assessment of the role of Russia and its rulers and leaders in the history of Belarus. But in general, the majority of the Belarus population shows its traditional tolerance, and inter-ethnic relations are basically friendly with all ethic groups enjoying the same rights and abiding by the same laws. Furthermore the level of 'Russification' of many Belarussians is so high (particularly in urban areas) that at the grass-roots there are no palpable differences to be observed.

Ethnic Poles make up the third biggest ethnic group in Belarus after Belarussians and Russians (about 500,000 people, or about 5 percent of the entire population). The Poles have been living in Belarus since very early times. Most of the Poles are Catholics. Ethnic Poles are more or less evenly scattered throughout Belarus but the greatest concentration of them is to be found in the western parts of the country (Grodno, Brest, Minsk, and Vitebsk *oblasts*). Among the urban population of Belarus the ethnic Poles constitute up to 5 percent, but in some town in western Belarus (Grodno, Lida, Postava, Mosty) and in Minsk this percentage is much higher.

The number of ethnic Poles in Belarus has fluctuated throughout the years: for example in 1897 the figure was 130,000 and in 1939 it went up to 1.3 mln. These fluctuations in the Polish ethnic population can be explained by immigration from Poland to Belarus and vice versa, Stalinist purges and repressions, and by forcible evictions to Russia and Central Asia. Since 1959 the Polish element in the population has been decreasing (from 6.7 percent down to 4.2 percent), which can be partially explained by changes in ethnic self-identification. According to the census of 1979, for example, out of 403,200 Poles in Belarus only 31,200 called Polish their native language; 298,400 claimed Belarussian as their native language and the rest considered Russian to be their mother tongue. A similar situation was observed until the mid-80s. The government used it to introduce discrimination against ethnic Poles in general and Catholics in particular since it was intent on real or formal assimilation (if your passport said you were Belarussian you were supposed to be one regardless what you considered yourself to be); the pressure of 'Belarussification' and 'Russification' (to a lesser extent) increased. Often enough, children born into mixed Polish-Belarussian families were registered as Belarussians, against the will of the parent or without their consent. These children typically grew up feeling neither Polish nor Belarussian, or had a split identity. Almost all the groups of Polish population have been assimilated into the Belarussian environment but many individuals still retain dialectical differences in their speech, cultural traditions, psychological features, *mores* of everyday life, religion. All of these things allow ethnic Poles to ethnically identify themselves as Poles but in their majority they are not prone to separatism or 'Great-Polish' chauvinism.

Until recent times ethnic Poles who knew Polish preferred to use it only in church or related spheres, but in the last few years the younger generations of ethnic Poles in Belarus have begun to study Polish, Polish history and Polish culture in a more determined manner. Today, about 13 percents of ethnic Poles in Belarus can speak Polish fluently and the number of those who use Polish in everyday life is growing. Several factors may have contributed to this growth: policies of the Polish government and of the Catholic Church of Poland; activities of Polish communities in Belarus and of educational and cultural societies (for example, *Polonia* in Minsk, *Traugut* in Brest, *Mickiewicz* in Grodno).

In 1990 all Polish communities in Belarus united into the Union of Poles of Belarus with a membership of about 22,000 and branches in all major towns. The Union aims at reviving the Polish language among all ethnic Poles of Belarus, supporting the wide use of the Belarussian language (as an official state language) and promoting Belarussian culture[26]. In recent years the number of schools with instruction in Polish has grown somewhat; Polish-language newspapers are regularly delivered to Belarus or published locally; Polish-language TV and radio broadcasts from Poland are transmitted by local stations. Free movement across the Belarus-Poland border, frequent contacts between relatives also contributed greatly to the revival of the Polish language in Belarus.

The process of revival of the Polish language and culture in Belarus is affecting Catholic Belarussians as well, many of whom have become almost indistinguishable in their habits, culture and language from ethnic Poles and have a double ethnic self-identification. The active role of the Catholic Church in Belarus annoys the Belarussian nationalist-fundamentalists who regard every ethnic Pole as a Belarussian who 'has gone Polish'. Some of the extremist Catholic clergymen take a diametrically opposite position, and regard every Catholic in Belarus, irrespective of his ethnic background, as a Pole. It is also very characteristic that most of the

26 *Kul'tura* 1994, no. 11 (16 March).

Catholic clergy reacted highly negatively to a wish expressed by some parishes to conduct their religious services in Belarussian[27] .

Up to 1939, in Western parts of Belarus Orthodox Christians were generally looked upon as 'Russians', and Catholics as 'Poles'. Such an attitude is still prevalent at the grass-roots level. This leads to a situation where the concept 'Belarussian', which is a second self-identification for many groups of Catholics and Orthodox Christians, plays nation-wide an integrating role, with religious affiliation being of secondary importance and not being dominant in choosing or determining one's titular nationality.

In general, different religious groups of population show tolerance in their relations and enjoy the same constitutional rights. In fact, equality has been gained only recently and some problems have emerged in relations between neighbouring congregations of different religious confessions. Catholics, for example, in a number of instances, have demanded that certain churches that had some time ago been given to the Orthodox Christians be returned to them. But all in all relations of ethnic Poles and Belarussians (Orthodox Christians, Catholics, Uniates and Protestants) are peaceful and good-neighbourly. The same can be said about relations between ethnic Poles and ethnic Russians, Russified Belarussians and other ethnic groups of Belarus.

The situation is somewhat destabilised (so far only to a small extent) by those Catholic clergymen who stubbornly pursue a policy of assimilating all Catholics into the Polish language and culture, that is to polonise them; and also by nationalist-fundamentalists who deny the importance of the Polish ethnic self-consciousness and identity and try to prove that all ethnic Poles in Belarus are in fact Polonised Belarussians. These opposing extremist views are shared today by relatively few people and are not officially supported today through the creation of a Polish enclave in Belarus or a Belarussian enclave in Poland or other similar measures. But in the eastern parts of Belarus where certain groups of Russian ethnics clamour for reunification with Russia, desire on the part of ethnic Poles to affirm their identity may potentially lead to conflicts; the excessive Belarussian ethnocentrism can also become a destabilising factor (Belarussian ethnocentrism can only be justified as a 'language and culture missionising' in its own ethnic environment).

---

27 Today, only at a few Catholic Churches of Belarus, religious services are held and sermons are delivered in the Belarussian language; at some churches two languages are used alternately (one day Polish, and the next day Belarussian) but in most churches a compromised approach is practiced: liturgy is conducted in Polish and sermons are delivered in Belarussian.

Ukrainians constitute the fourth largest ethnic (after Belarussians, Russians and Poles) group in Belarus, with about 300,000 people, or approximately 2.9 percent of today's Belarus population[28]. In ancient times, some of the ethnic groups (*Volynyane*, *Drevlyane*) which contributed to the subsequent formation of the Ukrainian ethnos, lived in some of the southern border areas of Belarus. A major influx of Ukrainian migrants into Belarus was observed in the 19th and early 20th centuries. The biggest groups settled in Pinsk, Brest, Gomel'', Rechitsk, Slutsk, Bobruysk, and Bykov *povets* [administrative regions]. In the second half of the 20th centuries immigration of rural Ukrainians virtually ceased and was supplanted by new Ukrainian immigrants from predominantly urban areas (workers, clerks, intellectuals, bureaucrats).

Ukrainians are more or less evenly scattered throughout the territory of Belarus, but a more compact Ukrainian population lives in parts of the country that are adjacent to Ukraine (Pinsk, Kobryn, Brest, Gomel'' and other southern regions). Most of those who call themselves 'Ukrainians' are, if they are believers, Orthodox Christians, but there are Catholics and Protestants among ethnic Ukrainians as well.

The *Poles'e* part of Belarus, a transition zone between Ukrainians and Belarussians, has many ethnographic and language peculiarities, and ethnic distinctions here are hardly observable. Local dialects are a mixture of Ukrainian, Belarussian and other languages, and sound very peculiar, so much so that neighbouring Belarussians and Ukrainians do not regard them as related to their own languages. This area's traditional culture, everyday-life styles, and psychology are also very easily distinguishable and different from those of the neighbours.

Some time ago inhabitants of this area, recognising these differences, called themselves either *poleshchuki* (those who spoke dialects which stand closer to the Ukrainian language) or *litviny* (those who spoke dialects which stand closer to the Belarussian language). Later, following the political events of the first half of the 20th century, inhabitants of one and the same area and members one of the same ethnic group used to get themselves registered either as 'Belarussians' or 'Ukrainians'. This led to a lot of confusion and many people experienced difficulties in trying to define their ethnic identify. Today, in Belarussian *Poles'e* one can find settlements where the people speak a dialect that is closer to the Ukrainian language rather then to Belarussian, but have 'Belarussian' written down in their internal passports; and alternatively, settlements where dialects are spoken that are more akin

---

28 According to the information of the Ukrainian Embassy, the number of Ukrainians in Belarus is several times this figure. *Belarus* 1994, no. 8.

to Belarussian, yet where people are registered (in their passports) as 'Ukrainians'[29]. That is why it is hard for many inhabitants of the area to determine their ethnic identify and in most cases the ethnic background only of one of the parents is regarded as sufficient in determining one's ethnic identify.

In recent years this has prompted local intellectuals to come out with an idea of having Poles'e establish itself as an autonomous unit with the view of integrating its population into a single cultural and language formation different from the rest of the country. A cultural-education society called *Palis'sya* was set up, a new literary language, based on one of the dialects, was created; some books and a periodical (*Zbudzinne* [Revival]) were published in this newly created language; it was planned to introduce it to the local schools as the language of instruction; and the local inhabitants were to be called *poleshchuk-yatsvygi*. This movement caused a controversy in Belarus. The Belarussian nationalist radicals opposed this idea, especially as far as a new autonomy was concerned. The local population did not support this idea either.

Recently the *Poles'e* cultural and language movement has split but the idea of preserving cultural and language peculiarities of Polissye has not been abandoned ('Poles'e Song Festivals' are regularly held, ethnographic museums are set up, folklore is being recorded, etc.). But there are some outstanding issues to be resolved. One of these concerns the language of instruction in local schools. Locals, regardless of the nationality they are registered under in their passports ('Belarussian' or 'Ukrainian') do not want to have their children being taught in Belarussian, but at the same time they do not do anything to have schools with instruction in Ukrainian, instead preferring to speak Russian and have their children taught in Russian. That is why most of the *Poles'e* ethnic Ukrainians are Russian-speaking or bilingual, using local dialects.

This is not the case with the Ukrainians who came to Belarus from Ukraine after 1945. They have their clearly established ethnic identity, and the Ukrainian language is one of the main features that links them with their Ukrainian ethnicity. The *Vatra* Association of Ukrainians in Belarus, established recently and made up mostly of recent immigrants, proclaims in its charter various aims which include teaching the Ukrainian language, publication of books on Ukrainian history and culture,

---

29 This possibly explains the difference in estimates of number of Ukrainians in Belarus, and the Ukrainian embassy's spokesmen regard all the groups of Western Polessye, whose dialects are close to the Ukrainian language, as potential Ukrainians an who might wish to by registered as Ukrainians.

upholding Ukrainian traditions, educating ethnic Ukrainians in the spirit of appreciation of Ukrainian language literature and Ukrainian language.

The *Vatra* Association includes several local societies (*Prosvita*, *Zapovit*, *Obriy* and others) which function in the areas with the greatest compact numbers of Ukrainians (Brest, Gomel'', and Minsk *oblasts*). In Minsk the Ukrainian Uniate congregation is allowed to use the local Uniate Cathedral for their services. In contrast to the *Poles'e*-born ethnic Ukrainians, most of these post-1945 Ukrainian immigrants show respect towards the Belarussian language and many of them even prefer to speak Belarussian rather than Russian.

The natural relations between Ukrainians and Belarussians are friendly and good-neighbourly and conflicts originating from national differences are extremely unlikely. Relations at the government level between Ukraine and Belarus are also good, and attempts by some nationalist-fundamentalist in the Ukraine to raise the question about changing the territorial status-quo in southern areas of Brest *oblast'* (Western *Poles'e*) did not find any response either at the government level or at the grass-roots level among ethnic Ukrainian living in these areas.

Jews are the next largest ethnic (to be more precise: ethnic-religious) group in Belarus. Their number is constantly decreasing because of their active emigration to Israel and other countries. In the last few year the number of Jews emigrating from Belarus began to fall (24,000 in 1990, 15,000 in 1991, 3400 in 1992 and 2500 in 1993). According to information supplied by the Israeli embassy, there are about 100,000 Jews living in Belarus today[30]. Jews have been living in Belarus since very early times. There are no Jewish enclaves in Belarus but most Jews live in urban areas. They speak mostly Russian; bilingual Jews, who can communicate in Yiddish as well as in Russian, are to be found mostly among elderly people. However, thanks to the introduction of Hebrew into Jewish schools, bilingualism is gaining new ground.

Jews in Belarus are the group of the population with the highest level of education. Among them one can find many engineers, physicians, teachers, lawyers, scholars, scientists, and musicians. This high level of education also implies a good knowledge of Belarussian among considerable numbers of Jewish people. They are well assimilated culturally in the Belarussian ethnic environment. During years of

---

30 According to census of 1989 there were 112,000 Jews in Belarus, that is 1.1 per cent of the entire population. Discrepancies in figures – 112,000 In 1989, 45,000 emigrated in 1990-1993, and today the estimated number of Jews living in Belarus, is about 100,000 – can be explained by the natural growth migrations, differences in what passports said regarding nationality and actual nationality, mixed marriages etc.

discrimination against the Jews in the USSR in general, and in the Belarussian SSR in particular (this discrimination had never been official but in had not made in any easier), this assimilation, mostly Russification, led to the loss by very many Jewish people of their traditional culture, religion and habits.

Because of their life in a non-Jewish environment, the Jews in their majority have lost knowledge of Yiddish and Hebrew, and anti-Semitism has made many of them change their nationality at the time of registration ('nationality' is entered in internal passports). This process began soon after 1945 and continued up to the mid-80s, and involved very many children born into families of mixed ethnic backgrounds, who preferred to be registered as 'Russians', 'Belarussians' or 'Ukrainians' thus avoiding being teased and laughed at at school, opening up the way to a prestigious college, to a more successful career, and giving a chance of travelling abroad. A double identity in this case was the result of unfavourable circumstances and a defensive step by the people who were discriminated.

It should be noted here that anti-Semitism had not been traditional in Belarus and that in became wide-spread only in mid-20th. century. Traditional Belarussian folklore tales are devoid of any traces of anti-Semitism; with usurers and money-lenders being the only group of population towards whom the attitude was unfriendly. In the early 20th century, two Jewish pogroms took place in Belarus and they were instigated by extremists (*chernosotentsy* [Black Hundred Righists]) who had come from St. Petersburg. Traditionally relations between Jews and other ethnic groups in Belarus had been good-neighbourly, both sides showing much tolerance. In recent times, after years of strained relations, the situation has begun to improve again shifting back to the original atmosphere of tolerance and friendliness where it no longer shameful to be called a Jew. This new atmosphere has been accompanied by a revival of ethnic identity and self-consciousness among the Jews who also show a heightened interest in Jewish history, culture, religion and tradition. The Belarussian Association of Jewish Communities and Organisations was established at a conference held in January of 1993 with as its main aim to promote the revival of the Jewish national, religious and cultural heritage. The Association unites more than a hundred different organisations (religious, scientific, educational and athletic). About a dozen Jewish Sunday schools are functioning in Belarus now with more than a thousand students attending them. In Minsk and Mogilev Jewish classes have been set up at up a regular secondary school and at art school; a number of synagogues have been opened in several towns of Belarus.

It should be mentioned here that the revival of Jewish cultural and religious life proceeds with practically no aid or budgetary assistance from the government. Such is the case for all other minority ethnic groups of Belarus, despite provisions in the 'National Minorities Law' which stipulate that Belarus must help „create the material conditions for developing education and culture... through allocation of the necessary sums of money from the state budget“[31]. It is obvious that the law finds no practical application, a situation that is fully understood by the leaders of all the ethnic councils that are carrying out educational and cultural work and that are obliged to seek financial support from foreign governments, organisations, the foreign diaspora and private persons.

The attitude of Lithuania can be cited hare as a characteristic example. According to official Belarussian sources there are about 7000 Lithuanians living in Belarus (the Embassy of Lithuania in Belarus claims there are more than 30,000[32]). Lithuania provides financial support for the education of ethnic Lithuanians in Belarus (there are two Lithuanian schools in Belarus), for the development of Lithuanian culture and upholding Lithuanian traditions (every village or town with a sufficient number of Lithuanians has a Lithuanian folklore dance-and-song group, books and newspapers, published in Lithuanian and the like).

Lithuanians live in all the parts of the country but in a number of areas there is a greater concentration of them (in the Ostovitsk and Voronovsk districts of Grodno *oblast'* and in the Braslav district of Vitebsk *oblast'*), and in some eastern areas of Belarus there are several settlements where Lithuanians constitute a majority, In general, Lithuanians are culturally assimilated in their Belarussian and Belarussian-Polish environment. Lithuanian is spoken mostly among the elderly people who studied it in their younger years; many of those who are considered to be Lithuanians have in fact ethnic backgrounds other than Lithuanian.

In early times, certain western areas of Belarus were inhabited by western Baltic population groups whose language was related to the Lithuanian. Most of this early population was assimilated into the Belarussian and Polish environments but some compact groups have managed to preserve their language, culture, habits, psychology and even their original ethnic names (*borti*, *dainova*, *sudavy*, *poleksyane* – Lithuanians call themselves *lietuvyai*). In Lithuania itself these

---

31 *Zvezda* 6 December 1993.

32 Discrepancies in the numbers of Lithuanians and Ukrainians as they appear in various sources can be explained by changes in 'passport nationality (that is nationality registered in passport.

Western Baltic ethnic groups were assimilated into the Lithuanian ethnic environment back in the 40s and 50s of the 20th century, but in Belarus this has not happened and one can say that the Lithuanian influence upon these groups has been diminishing (for example, in 1957 there were eight Lithuanian schools in the Ostrovetsk and Voronovsk districts while in 1987 there functioned only one).

This western Baltic population in Belarus is not certain about their ethnic identity. They believe they are related to Lithuanians because of their language („which resembles Lithuanian“) and because the territory where they live once was called *Litva* (i.e., Lithuania; and this is accurate). It is likely that these groups can preserve their ethnicity only if they are Lithuanianised. This is helped by the fact that there has been a considerable immigration of Lithuanians from Lithuania into Belarus in recent decades, some of it permanent, some of it temporary. Religious services in churches are conducted in Lithuanian (sometimes in Lithuanian and Polish); most of the western Baltic population in Belarus, like the Lithuanians themselves, are Catholics. Migrant Lithuanians, local ethnic Lithuanians and the 'Lithuanianised' western Baltic population tend to preserve their ethnicity even in marriages with other ethnics, (including marriages with Slavs). Relation of Lithuanians and related groups with Belarussian and other ethnic groups are good-neighbourly with both sides respecting each other (respect is a characteristic feature of Lithuanians in general).

The Lithuanians are earnestly respectful towards the issues of national revival of Belarussians, towards Belarussian language and culture. The 'Belarus-Litva' Society, recently established, promotes cultural contacts between Lithuanians and Belarussians; the Lithuanian *Sajudis* national-patriotic organisation is an ally of the BNF; a number of Belarussian schools has been opened in Lithuania. No inter-ethnic conflicts of Lithuanians with Belarussians or any other ethnic groups are known to have ever taken place. Attempts of Lithuanian national-fundamentalists and some Lithuanian officials to bring about a revision of the existing borders are being dealt with at the diplomatic level.

Tatars constitute another ethnic group that has always been playing a certain role in inter-ethnic relations in Belarus. Today they number about 13,000 people (according to the census of 1970 there were about 10,000 Tatars in Belarus). Tatars in Belarus, descendants of Kyptchak Turkic tribes along the Northern shores of the Black Sea, from the Crimea and Turkic people of Central Asia, have been living in Belarus since the 14th century. They are related to the ethnic Tatars in Lithuania and Poland with whom they maintain close cultural and religious relations. The Tatars in

Belarus are basically Sunni Muslims but with some peculiarities in their religious and every-day life (for example they are all monogamous). Some Tatars had been converted into Christianity and were easily assimilated; other continued to uphold theirs ethnicity through religiously ordained endogamy. The Tatars in Belarus do not spear their Turkic language and dialects (they lost knowledge of it a very long time ago), but their active acculturation and assimilation (belarussianisation and polonisation) did not start until the 20th century. Today ethnic Tatars speak Russian or Belarussian, although the language of the religious services in the mosques remains Arabic. Tatars are dispersed more or less evenly throughout Belarus but there are relatively compact Tatar settlements in the Grodno, Novogrudsk, Brest, Gomel'', Cherven, Vitebsk, Ivyevsk, Mogilev and Minsk regions.

At the end of the 80s the process of Tatar national revival began with the creation of a Tatar association in Belarus and Lithuania. In 1991 the local Tatar association was reorganized to become the *Al-Qitab* [Holy Book] Association of Muslim Tatars of Belarus. In 1993 the Muslim Religious Association of Belarus came into being uniting 25 Muslim religious communities of Belarus. Efforts are being made to integrate, on a cultural and religious basis, the Muslim Tatars of Belarus, Lithuania and Poland, but the leaders of the Tatars of Belarus believe that their main task is to preserve their ethnic identity, revive Islam culture and Muslim religion. It is planned to celebrate the 600th anniversary of Tatar settlement in Belarus and in Lithuania in 1997.

Today, there is only one mosque functioning in Belarus in the town of Iv'e where a Muslim cultural centre is also being built, and in Dovbush and Novogrudka old mosques are being repaired (several mosques will have been built before the celebrations in 1997). Most of the Tatars in Belarus (young people in particular) have little knowledge of the traditional faith of their ancestors, are not fanatically religious and are religiously tolerant (Muslim religious leaders are constantly calling for tolerance). No religious or ethnic fundamentalism is known to exist at a group level among the Tatars in Belarus; the Tatar cultural-religious elite are not only sympathetic to the Belarussian revival movement but even participate in it.

Other ethnic groups in Belarus are numerically small and do not play any noticeable role in inter-ethnic relations in Belarus, adding only some specific features. According to the information of the Committee on National Policies and Inter-National Relations in the Supreme Soviet of the Republic of Belarus, all in all there are more than 100 groups of various ethnic backgrounds in Belarus. Among the larger groups, both autochthonous and those who have settled down in Belarus in recent decades, one can find Latvians, Gypsies, Czechs, Slovaks, Germans, Armenians, Azerbaidzhani, Hungarian, Koreans, Greeks, Estonians, Ossetians, Georgians and others. Some of them have established their cultural, religious, educational, folklore, ethnographic societies (for example: the Belarussian centre of German culture, the Armenian Cultural Society, the Korean Cultural society; the Roma Cultural and Folklore Club in Vitebsk and others).

Migration processes that have picked up steam in recent years lead to the reduction of some groups (Latvians, Estonians, Greeks, Germans and some others) and increases in the numerical strengths of others (mostly because of the influx of refugees from troubled areas within the borders of the former Soviet Union: Armenians, Azerbaidzhani, Ossetians, Georgians and others). Emigration from Belarus is mostly motivated by economic reasons and family reunion. By contrast, Belarus attracts immigrants because of its image of a country where inter-ethnic relations are peaceful, friendly and good-neighbourly, with a high level of tolerance. All the issues and problems of all ethnic groups in Belarus are to be dealt with and solved by the Committee on National Minorities of the cabinet of Ministers of the Republic of Belarus, but this Committee, which functions within the structure of the highest executive power, is not able to do all it is supposed to do because of lack of financing from the state budget.

Several non-profit public organisations have recently decided to establish a Centre of National Cultures, whose main aim would be to promote the type of national relations that are characteristic for multi-national developed states of the West. It should be mentioned that at the grass-roots level such relations have been established in Belarus a long time ago. At the governmental level a lot more attention is to be paid to the maintenance of normal and equal inter-ethnic relations. We would like to conclude this essay on ethnic and national relations in Belarus by mentioning priorities in the list of the things to be done yet. The Belarussian national idea today is weak and is not widely supported in society, with only 10-15 % per cent backing it. There is a certain section of the Belarus population that for various reasons sides with the nationally oriented population, attracted by the idea of consolidation within the system of an ethnic nation. However, because of the deficiencies in ethno-sociological research it is difficult to establish the percentage of these sympathisers with any definitive results and it can be ascertained only by indirect means.

Besides the Belarussians themselves the ideas of a Belarussian national revival are mostly supported by ethnic Ukrainians, Lithuanians, Tatars, and to a lesser extent by ethnic Russians and other ethnic groups most of which view these ideas with indifference or even reject them. The ideas of creating a civic-territorial or pluralistic nation in Belarus have currency only among local provincial Belarussian and other ethnic leaders. Inter-ethnic relations are basically determined by traditional and new Belarussian-Russian-Polish relations in which, because of Belarussian nationalism and Russian and Polish chauvinism, conflict-stimulating tendencies are starting to become stronger. Such tendencies are only latent among the majority of population in Belarus but are rather more pronounced among national and ethnic elites.

10

List of Authors

Chakvin, Igor' Vsevolodovich (1954, Minsk), ethnographer and ethnologist, doktor of history; senior researcher at the Belarussian Academy of Sciences' Institute of Fine Arts, Ethnography and Folklore.

Fabel, Frank (1962), graduated in social history from (West)Berlin University; free-lancer with radio RIAS-Berlin; lives in Russia since 1992; head of bureau of the St.Petersburg based German-Russian Exchange organization (NGO).

Golovakha, Evgenii Ivanovich (1950, Kiev), social scientist; Institute of Sociology of the Ukrainian Academy of Sciences.

Kolossov, Vladimir Aleksandrovich (1953, Moscow), doktor of geography, specialized in economic geography of foreign countries; head of the Center for European Geopolitical Research at the Russian Academy of Sciences' Institute of Geography.

Kozlov, Vladimir Nikolaevich (1955, Moscow), kandidat of geographic sciences; fellow at the Russian Academy of Sciences' Institute of Geography, laboratory for human ecology; leading specialist with the department for regional research at the analytical center of the Russian public television ORT (*Obshchestvennoe Rossiiskoe televidenie*).

Makarov, Anatolii Vasil'evich (1945, Slutsk), professor and prorector of the Belarussian Institute of Higher Education and Humanitarian Sciences.

Novogrodskii, Tadeush Antonovich (1965, Grodno oblast'/Belarus'), historian, ethnographer, ethnologist; junior researcher at the Belarussian Academy of Sciences' Institute of Fine Arts, Ethnography and Folklore.

(continued on next page)

Panina, Natal'ya Viktorovna (1949, Sochi), social scientist; Institute for Sociology of the Ukrainian Academy of Sciences.

Treivish, Andrei Il'ich (1950, Moscow), geographer specialized in economic and social geography; fellow at the Russian Academy of Sciences' Institute of Geography, contributer to the department for regional research at the analytical center of the Russian public television ORT (*Obshchestvennoe Rossiiskoe televidenie*).

Voronkov, Viktor Mikhailovich (1945, Leningrad), sociologist; director of the St. Petersburg Center for Independent Research.

11

Index

A

B

C

D

E

F

G

H

I

J

K

N

O

P

R

S

T

U

V

W

Y

Z

12

Cumulative Table of Contents

Klaus Segbers (Hrsg.)

Rußlands Zukunft: Räume und Regionen

Dieses Buch widmet sich einer der heute zentralen Fragen in Rußland: dem Erwachen der 88 »Subjekte der Föderation« und der – bei Einbeziehung der Kosakentümer und einiger Wehrkreise – über 100 regionalen Einheiten Rußlands. Die Ursachen des wachsenden, mitunter explodierenden Selbstbewußtseins der Regionen und des Strebens nach Erhöhung ihres Status sind vielfältig und haben zunächst wenig mit Ethnokonflikten zu tun. Zahlreiche Faktoren haben dazu geführt, daß der Bestand der Russischen Föderation nicht mehr gesichert ist: die irrationale territoriale Abgrenzung der Republiken und Regionen; das Bestreben nationaler Eliten, sich auf »Staatssuche« zu begeben; der Kampf um Ressourcen; der Druck der Bevölkerung, die ihre materiellen Ansprüche an lokale und regionale Verwaltungen richtet.

Die Beiträge 14 russischer und zwei westlicher Autoren thematisieren u.a.: Voraussetzungen, Ursachen und Verlaufsformen von Autonomisierung und Regionalisierung, die traditionelle Regionalpolitik Rußlands; die materiellen Transfers zwischen Zentrum und Regionen und zwischen Regionen; die Wanderungsbewegungen der Bevölkerung. Fünf Regionalstudien und zwei Untersuchungen über »Rußland und der Islam« und die »Russische Idee« runden die Darstellung ab.

1994, 277 S., brosch., 33,– DM, 232,50 öS, 30,– sFr,
ISBN 3-7890-3282-4
(Aktuelle Materialien zur Internationalen Politik, Bd. 33)